Say What?!

'What' You Say is Your Future!

Second Edition

Tarshish Productions
Elkhart, Indiana

Linda C. Newberry

Copyright 1-863234131 © 2012 by Linda C. Newberry

All rights reserved. Written permission must be secured from the publisher to use or reproduce any part of this book, except for brief quotations in critical reviews or articles.

Published by Tarshish Productions, 1933 N Stone Maple Lane, Elkhart, Indiana 46514.

Unless otherwise noted, Scripture quotations are taken from the King James Bible.

References to Strong's concordance are taken from the Strong's Exhaustive concordance in both book and electronic form.

ISBN 978-1-941201-01-5

www.lindacnewberry.com
Printed in the United States of America

Table of Contents

Acknowledgements 9

Introduction 11

Wake Up and Smell the Coffee 21

It Ain't Over, 'til it's Over! 37

Come Gather 'Round! 43

Support: Giving and Receiving It 53

Wealth from Many Lands 61

Hasty Fruit? That's Promising! 71

Money Ministry....Helping Those in Need 81

Discerning the Needs of Others 91

Tarshish: To Satisfy Every Debt 97

The Gift of Other Peoples Harvest 107

Who Left the Gate Open? 117

Are You Being Served? 127

Character Traits – Elements of Success 137

The Great Turn-Around 145

Victory Without End! 153

Extraordinary Provision 161

No Matter How Small, God Will Use It 167

Peace At Last! 175

You Are My Sunshine 181

Grieve No More 189

It Is Not About You Anyway 195

It's Harvest Time! 203

Conclusion 209

Isaiah 60 Confession 213

Acknowledgements

The first thank you goes to, Erika Jackson, my dear friend. I appreciate your helping me to see that this information would be of interest and help to others. Many thanks go to the people who mentored me behind the scenes. Most do not know me, however, I have listened and taken to heart your teachings over the last two decades.

You have given me the courage to dream bigger....reaching for things and acting on ideas that were in the past always blocked by lack of confidence and paralyzing fear. Although 'failure' in ventures has happened more than once, I've learned that falling, failing is not fatal...as a matter of fact it is a part of the success process. The difference in how you see, understand and label 'failing' is key to moving forward. If it hadn't been for the teachings of so many that had gone before me...I would never have tried again. If I had not tried again I'd never had the successes that have come my way.

I place more stock in the ideas that flow to me now than I did before I met you. Because of your teachings and encouragement, I am not afraid to investigate and develop new ideas. You have inspired me to strive for excellence in character, actions and relationships....and although I have not 'arrived'....the important point to focus on is that I'm better than I once was and working toward being a better person as the days go by. You have given me information needed to understand my connection with God, and His desire for me to live life. By listening to your stories and following your example you have helped me to see that I could be more.

In closing, thanks go to my family. My parents and siblings who even when they may have thought I was crazy stood behind me and spurred me on to stretch myself, grow and produce what was in my mind and heart. I love you guys and will be forever grateful because you have believed in me during the bad times and celebrated with me in the good. Thanks for your love and support.

My love and gratitude,
Linda

Introduction

Nothing splendid has ever been achieved except by those who dared believe that something inside of them was superior to circumstance.   Bruce Barton

Grab a cup of coffee, bottle of water or soda and settle in for heart changing information. Questioning yourself is locating you. The first thing God said to Adam and Eve after they had eaten the fruit was 'Where art thou?' So throughout this book there will be questions that hopefully help you to see where you are in comparison to where you want to be. Let's get started.

Are you consumed by current conditions and circumstances? Has complacency set in with dread that somehow tomorrow will not be any different than today or yesterday? Don't be dismayed!

The world we live in is a strange and wonderful place. You were placed here on this earth for a reason. Your presence here means you have a purpose right here, right now.

Hopelessness seems promoted in our society. It seems to be all around us, but you do not have to fall into that trap. If you have found yourself in that pit, I want you to know that you don't need to stay there. You have a way out. Picking up this book is not a coincidence.

"Say What?!..." is a book that will open your eyes to see that there is more to this life God designed for you. If you absorb this information, allow your mind and heart to wrap around it and then act on it, it can change in your life.

Although you may not yet know what your purpose is, you are here on this earth, in this country, in your town; your company or your family "for such a time as this." Your personality, talents and skills put you in a position to do something and make an impact in a way that no one else can.

Your dreams are real. Your experiences, the way you talk, think and act will open the doors of opportunity that have been uniquely designed for you to discover. You have the ability and right to have what you have dreamed. However, successful living takes work, and diligent attention. Success is never just handed to you on a silver platter.

In order to make any headway, you will have to "take the trash out" of your life. You may find that your head and heart are filled with confusing and contradictory information. In our era of technology, we are inundated with emails, advertisements and articles. Day by day, we are told by people who have no tolerance for views other than their own, that it is not sufficient to accept that they have different views and agree to disagree.

Instead, they attempt to force us to embrace their views. Fear attempts to oppress you with conformity. Conformity squashes uniqueness. If you have not developed an understanding of who you are and what you are here for, and when pushed and pulled by so many varying views; confusion cannot help but be present.

One of the by-products of confusion is feeling out of control. Have you felt helplessness, believing "it is what it is" and that nothing can change it? This comes from attempting to soak in too many opposing viewpoints and make them your own. There are several industries whose livelihoods depends on swaying your view; adding to the confusion.

Early in life your family's morals and/or set of beliefs was the major source of shaping the heart and mind of the person you have become. Then there was education. In days of old you went to school to be taught the skills to make it in the world. The morals taught at home were reinforced there; developing in the student a strong sense of character and integrity.

Today's educational system has changed greatly. In the same school that years ago Biblical principles and clean living were upheld are now being forced to teach political correctness, the theme that there are no losers, and everyone is a winner.

Baloney! We have been programmed to conform by our educational system, our government and, unfortunately, sometimes even our families unwittingly took part in this programming. Strangely many leaders say they are promoting diversity and accepting differences, the promotion of these diversities is at the expense of the freedoms of those who do not agree with them.

Freedom of speech and thought is feared rather than embraced. I urge you to use your imagination. Open your mind and think. Think bigger than ever before. Don't fall prey to corrupt programming. Make a stand for your life and your family. I have a feeling that deep inside you this is making sense.

We desire freedom, justice and interaction. Decisions are being made for many of us against our will all in the name of taking care of us. These outside circumstances fuel fear and amplify the feeling of powerlessness. BUT feeling powerless is an illusion.

Although many people fall prey to this fear and allow these feelings to rule their life, to make them lazy; you can choose a different and more productive path. If hearing this information makes something in your spirit leap, that is HOPE! Hang onto it, fuel it and promote it!

"Say What?!..." will help you to see the difference between what you see is what you get (allowing yourself to be a victim of life) and what you say is what you get (learning and knowing that you are able to respond to the circumstances that attempt to keep you inactive…you are response-able for change in your life). Make a break.

Break out of any mold you have been conforming to out of obligation, because of someone else's expectations or due to fear. Change the way you talk about yourself and the things happening in your life.

Inappropriate labels and negative tapes reinforce the idea that you can only go so far or that you are unable to move to make a change. Instead of letting the negative chapters of your past and even those current circumstances label you incorrectly, instead of allowing other people in your life to place a name tag on you; take back your authority, take back that responsibility and begin to ***"Say What?!..."*** you desire to be the life you see.

Be strong, you were born strong…strong in mind and heart. It is time for you to make some changes and one of the best moves you can make; take a stand for you, your family and your country! Choose to name the situation, name the past, and name yourself.

Make those choices yourself. Do not let anyone place a name on you that does not fit. And if what "they" are saying about you is or was true, you have the ability to change.

It can be a challenge to change the way you think and speak about yourself, but I believe in you. This is a challenge for which you were born. You have the power to make your life the one about which you have always dreamed.

Now, let's talk money. How much is enough? If you were to ask that question of a hundred people and you would hear a hundred different answers. You might even find some people who have never given this enough thought to give you an answer.

Some believe that they need only enough for their families, just them, their spouse and children. Getting by is the status quo, and that is okay with them. In many cases, people have been born into deep poverty, and that poverty is so deeply imbedded in their thinking that they believe that this lifestyle is their only option.

In many cases, religious ideas have shaped poverty based beliefs. The idea here may sound something like this; to be spiritual means that a person is required to live in poverty, barely "scraping by." And yet in other cases, it is a struggling parent who is doing their best to provide for their children's basic needs, who downplay the benefits of financial stability and increase, maybe even to the point of suggesting that the higher road was operating in poverty.

You may have heard, "money doesn't make you happy." And, of course you want to be happy…RIGHT? In the mind of a small child listening to this statement, it could translate; "...poverty is not only okay but, maybe even necessary for happiness to exist." After all, money does not lead to the ultimate goal of happiness.

Or, you may have heard, "make sure you marry for love and not money." The insinuation being that love and money don't or can't exist in the same relationship.

As well-meaning as these statements may have been, and were probably handed out to protect their children from disappointment, and it is true that money doesn't equal happiness; we know the opposite is an equally unbalanced thought.

Poverty certainly doesn't equal happiness either, and carries its own set of problems. Happiness and joy come from a solid foundation and can be found in either situation. It is that foundation that will allow you to handle properly the wealth that comes your way.

By the way, disappointments are a part of life and present all of us (children included) with opportunities to learn life lessons. In a parent's desire to protect their young one from hurt, these statements are offered. However, they are lopsided statements that plant seeds of hopelessness early in life.

Disappointment is not fatal, but often used as a building block for something better. Now the government has come into the schoolroom and home, dictating that disappointing situations be eliminated from everyday living.

Rules have been put in place so that everyone wins in competitions. They place constraints on achievers so that those who are not as successful don't feel bad about themselves. They are also attempting to put in place laws that penalize those who are financially successful; just a sick twist on the Robin Hood story.

Does any of this sound familiar? You probably know people who fit one of these categories. I think we can all agree; money alone does not bring happiness or guarantee a happy marriage; however, it does not preclude them either.

Others have either sidestepped this programming or have worked their way past the incongruities and have developed large scale dreams for their life. They desire not only enough to satisfy basic needs, but enough to help those in need. It is important to understand that if all you bring home is enough to care for your immediate family, your ability to give to worthy causes will be low or non-existent.

There are many rungs in the ladder between the poverty level and extreme wealth. Where do you stand on this ladder? Where do you want to be? There is no right or wrong answer here. Just locating.

"Say What?! ..." is not a book of formulas to get wealth from God. It is a book of word pictures of the way He planned for all of us to live. It talks about your personal presentation, provision no matter what the rest of society is

experiencing, how people will see you, your protection and the benefit you will be to those in your circle of influence.

I expect that once you are done reading these pages your mind will have been lifted out of some old mindsets and open to exploring new extraordinary possibilities. No matter where you stand today; money serves a couple of main purposes. The first is that it meets our basic needs Even the Bible states, "money answers all things." The second purpose is to be used as a means of helping other people.

Money if used properly is here to fulfill needs, both our personal needs and those of others that we encounter, often those who are less fortunate. There is probably no other thing on earth that can make a person feel better than to helping someone meet a need.

On each rung of this financial ladder, you will find people who are givers. The difference is in the magnitude of giving. If you do not have enough to take care of your basic needs, your focus is trying to get your own needs met. Without sufficient funds, you have a difficult time paying your bills and having food on the table. It is difficult to be generous, lighthearted and merry when your needs are not met.

Lack is an all-consuming, self-centered state. It screams for attention, and if unaware, you will cater to the screaming by focusing all of your attention on where you are, not where you are going. Even more so when someone places a need before you are you able to respond with assistance?

In the case of the hurricane in New Orleans, you may have wanted to help, but with limited resources you may only have been able to send a small amount. Is that all you wanted to do? Was it on your heart to send more or take time off to go to that area to help in clean-up efforts? Could you afford to take the time off work?

You could be making a lot of money and still stretched to the very limit financially, feeling just as helpless as a person who is on an hourly rate, in constant motion going nowhere. According to your reference point of enough, do you have it? Are you there yet? Or has it seemed an illusion that is always somehow just out of your grasp?

"Say What?!..." can help you break free, financially and otherwise. This book shows you in His words the life he has desired for you, and you will be amazed.

He loves you! However, if you are now wondering, "But, if this is so, why are so many people hurting?"; some of the answers can be found here. A serious lack of study time spent seeking truth, wrong perceptions and generations of teachings taken at face value without checking the source have helped create this gap between what could be and what is. Change your mindset, change your words, begin to take action on your dream and change your outcome.

Just like the quote above, dare to '...believe that something inside of you is superior to the circumstance' of your life. Take action on the words of **"Say What?! ..."** Begin to see your life change.

THE CONFESSION

I come today in dominion. I get up and decree-guaranteed success-sure success. I am luminous. My heart and mind are illuminated by Almighty God. The clear thinking, understanding, and happiness of the Lord are streaming from me. Lavish outpouring (glory) of the Lord is appearing upon me and in my life.

I am heavy with riches, I am heavy with abundance, I am heavy with the splendor of wealth, I am heavy with magnificent copiousness. *What does this mean to you? Personalize it with your idea of what this means for you.*

CHAPTER 1

Wake Up and Smell the Coffee

Isaiah 60:1
Arise, shine; for thy light is come, and the glory of the LORD is risen upon thee.

Arise and shine are amazing words when you look them up. Arise is just that; get up, get going, do something. Many of the problems I have seen in my own life and in the lives of those I have encountered are because there is a lack of movement. Sometimes this takes the form of physical movement, but often a lack of mental and spiritual movement, lack of gaining knowledge and understanding about the problem, a situation or about even about ourselves.

If you are a person who is always physically moving, sometimes you end up making things worse by reacting to your daily circumstances rather than responding. Reactions are impulsive acts. Very often they are unplanned with no thought of consequence. Responses are conscious acts, contemplated.

Being a responder instead of a reactor can be learned. If you find that you act impulsively to people and circumstances in your life, you can train yourself to handle these situations differently. You can change many of the things about you that you find unproductive and begin to produce fruit where you once thought it impossible.

Think of the exercise of driving. When you first begin the process of learning this skill you are operating strictly out of book knowledge and after much practice behind the wheel, you are trained. You begin operating in wisdom, and the process becomes almost instinctual. It no longer is difficult to do the right thing at the right time.

Arise! Get up and move, take action toward the dream you have in your heart. Take action in the form of thinking and opening your imagination, being creative and letting the ideas flow. Action is taking the time to plan how to bring the idea from thought to reality. Take each planned activity and action to walk out the plan.
Now, when you shine in your area of expertise, success is evident not only to you but to those around you. Success is your right as a man or woman of God. To live below that success is truly a crime against your creator. And you see, if God said it, it is guaranteed.

Success is not guaranteed to only to the learned. It is available for you if you believe. The only thing that can completely stop your progress is buying into the lies coming to you from the other camp. This enemy camp is any person, thought or circumstance that is used to come against you and your dream. That thing will try to stop you.

Some of the biggest problems you will encounter in your journey are not the current outside influences. Instead, they will be your own negative, demeaning and sometimes even crazy thought processes developed over the years. Now I'm not saying you are crazy, but if you are honest with yourself, don't you sometimes wonder "where in the world did that thought come from?"

It will be necessary to take control of those thoughts and replace them with thoughts and words that develop a picture in your mind of what you want to see happen. Just take a look in the pages of your Bible, and you will find loads of word pictures that will get you started.

It is important that you respond to the negative thoughts that come to you by speaking the opposite. The thing is, ideas are great, but multitudes of dreams die before they can be realized by the negative "stuff" going on in your own mind. Stop it! Counter the negative with life giving words.

"Say What ?! ... " you want to happen and then begin to do it! Your positive words trump any negative thought, the same way an ace trumps a jack in a card game. If you make a habit of basing those words on the promises found in the Bible; the power of agreement will also be working for you.

In my experience, more than anything else, people believe that God is more than able to do all the good in the

Bible. The question lingers, "But will He do it for me?" The problem with believing His promises arise in your feelings about yourself.

So much of what you are willing to do for someone and what they are willing to do for you depends on what is done to deserve the favor. We tend to filter our understanding of God on what we would do or how others have treated us. Take your understanding of what is possible not according to your experience, but take a chance and believe what He is saying.

The whole chapter of Isaiah 60 is a blueprint of what lies ahead for you, for us. Will you dare to believe that He sees you as described in these words? Will you choose to accept his vision of you, your abilities, your destiny, your standing in the community; right down to the possessions He has waiting for you?

You do not need to submit to and crumble under the weight of any circumstance. The blueprint is written. He works behind the scenes for you, gives you direction and courage, friends and supporters. Your part is to listen for and follow direction…..and shine.

You become luminous… you shine, as you allow Him in to give the direction and understanding needed to develop that seed of greatness He has placed within you. What is the dream that you have been dreaming? Spend time with Him; develop your dream. When you do, I believe that people will see the difference in you. You really will seem to shine, maybe not like what the Israelites saw when Moses came down from the mount, but people will see a difference when you are walking out your dream.

Glory is another great word that I had always taken as some super spiritual word; you couldn't see it, or touch it, word. And although it is a word that signifies a heavy presence and is often used Biblically to express God's physical presence; this is not the whole truth.

What you probably already know in your heart is that every lesson in both the Bible and everyday life have a natural or physical side to them, and a spiritual side. It is an opinion, but it seems that too often only the spiritual side of the lesson is taught in the Church; leaving the natural or physical meaning of the lesson on the sidelines .

I'm just throwing this thought out to contemplate. Would it make sense to you that a good Father would want his kids to be prepared only spiritually? Is it feasible to think he would have them living in a natural/physical environment, with no material preparation? Would it be kind and loving to have them equipped to think only lofty thoughts, while struggling in this environment because they are not physically, materially equipped to live in a physical world?

No. We need both. One won't work well without knowledge of the other. Segregating pieces of our life away from the spiritual connection means a disconnect to the power to succeed at your highest. They go hand-in-glove; they are flip sides of the same coin. So let's get back at it.

Glory is a very material word, also, meaning heaviness, lavish outpouring. This can be either material or spiritual; abundance, riches, splendor of wealth, and magnificent copiousness. He is very clear. "The glory of the Lord is risen upon thee." Thee…you!

You see, this is what I am talking about. Sometimes at this point your mind blanks out or may send you a thought like, "why would God's glory (abundance, riches, splendor of wealth, and magnificent copiousness) rise on me?" His glory (abundance, riches, splendor of wealth, and magnificent copiousness) may raise on someone who hasn't messed up the way that I have, but….not me. This is when you need to begin to ***"Say What?! ..."*** and exercise your faith.

The history behind Isaiah 60, full of promises, is that the Israelites had messed up big time, and for years. For years, they had been wishy-washy. Sin and a lax way of life, along with turning away from Him and then back again was something that they had experienced more than once.

At the time this was written; they were feeling as undeserving and removed as you may feel, at times. They were sorry for their inconsistency and the verses of this chapter were a not so gentle nudge for them, a reminder of what He had promised them. It is what he is saying to you now, not only individually but as a nation.

It's like "Hey guys! Get out there and be noticed for the people of integrity, honor and authority that I made you to be. Let your light shine, the glory I have placed in and on you for others to see. They will see and understand, just how much I love you and them.

Give those who don't know me something to look forward to. Be a shining example of the life I have always had planned for you. Let your talents and skills, your wisdom and good works shine in a world of darkness. Become what you are to become and take your place in the home, business and government. Be teachers, preachers, law makers and enforcers. Be scientists, inventors and authors.

Get married, raise your children and be faithful friends. Live your life like there is no tomorrow. Allow me to be central to your life. There is so much I want to show you and so many hours of exploration and fun beyond your wildest dreams. I have secrets that I want to share with only you, and things I want you to show others. I love you and have since the before the beginning of time.

And money? Understand that your walking with me will more than provide for everything you will ever need. Take me at my word…there are plenty of references to the supply I have for you, but you need to take them as yours…believe those words pertain to you. Now, guys, let's start to walk this thing out together!"

God loves pulling someone who will dare to believe out of a mess. Yes, even a mess of their own making and set him in this place of overwhelming good. Will you dare to believe that he not only *can* but *will* do for you what he has done for others? If you do begin to *"Say What ?! …"*

As you study the words used in the Bible, you will see that these words are very often financially based words. The true meanings or expanded meanings were often lost in the translation. For your studies, you can find the meanings of Hebrew and Greek words in the Strong's Concordance and many other reference guides. God talks so much about his people having more than enough financially. This is where you will need to stand firm against "old tapes" that attempt to side track you from your path to success.

Wake up and smell the coffee! He has a better life for you than you may realize. You give Him access by speaking the right words over your life, His words. You know the dream. Now find the words that support your dream and ***"Say What?! ..."***

Remember this: "My heart is indicting a good matter. I speak of the things which I have made touching the King; my tongue is the pen of a ready writer." Psalm 45:1

THE CONFESSION

Although there is darkness all around me, lavish outpouring is seen upon me and in my life by others.

CHAPTER 2

It Ain't Over, 'til it's Over!

Isaiah 60:2
For, behold, the darkness shall cover the earth, and gross darkness the people: but the LORD shall arise upon thee, and his glory shall be seen upon thee.

We face more danger than at any other time in the history. Terrorists are no longer attacking other shores, but are hitting us where we live. The attacks seem to be coming from within our government, as well. People seem to be in universal disagreement about most everything. Lines are drawn in the sand and sides are being taken.

People we have elected to do the will of "the people" have chosen to make up rules as they go and are disregarding the wants of the people they are supposed to be representing. This amounts to no less than an internal attack on our way of life. In days gone by, it would be called treasonous.

The life, the liberty that our forefathers died to win for us is slipping between our fingers. The people behind both the outward and internal attacks alike, hunger for power and position. This is darkness. This word so vividly describes the life we are experiencing now. Look at this definition: misery, destruction, death, ignorance, sorrow, wickedness, obscurity and night.

We face a multitude of diseases, some old and some new. They are deadly, insidious ailments and corroding afflictions; striking fears in the hearts of men. Although some of these diseases are very real, another threat is the propagation of the belief that prescription medications are the answer to every problem. Many of these create more issues than the ailments that they are supposed to be treating.

Doctors pile one medication on another on another, each with their own list of devastating side effects until the patient is overcome with affliction that could harm them forever or to the point of death. Simply put…people are over medicated. Why? Many people are not taking responsibility for the details of their lives.

People are not asking questions. They have become accustomed to having "help" from sources outside the family and church. They have leaned heavily on the government and the many agencies, departments and programs that have been constructed to "help." Many people depend on them to the point that they feel as though they can't do anything on their own anymore.

Why are they not gathering information so that they can wisely decide? They are allowing other people to do their thinking for them. They never ask the real cost, the hidden cost of all of this "help." This has come in the form of seemingly harmless programs and ideas penetrating our lives over several decades. Often they don't realize they are in the middle of it until it is too late. This is darkness.

Even the weather is stranger these days. Stories of torrential rains, tornados, hurricanes, tsunamis, drought, blizzards, earthquakes and erupting volcanoes populate the news. We are even seeing earthquakes in areas that normally have little to no seismic activities. Case in point, is the 3.6 earthquake that recently hit the Washington, D.C. area.

Catastrophic earthquakes, like the one that rocked Haiti in early 2010; they are still reeling from its effects. We cannot forget Japan and the incredible devastation the world is still feeling from the tsunami.

There are other strange happenings not necessarily related to weather. Well, we don't think so, anyway. Strange events like mass quantities of birds falling dead from the sky in numerous places in the world, in a specific time frame. This is darkness.

Crime seems to be more now than ever before, in concentration and severity. Crime was once thought of as a thing that was most frequently done by men, but now women and even children are at the heart of some of the most vicious attacks. In years gone by we never would have imagined that our schools would have metal detectors and security guards searching students before being admitted for classes.

This martial law setting at the entrances and exits of the public schools may protect the students and school staff, but does it infringe on basic human rights. Parents afraid for the safety of their children agree to this protocol in an attempt to protect them. Other parents are home schooling to keep their children safe and teach them the values that are no longer a part of the public education system. This is darkness.

Our financial markets have been unstable. Currencies have flip-flopped. Many people have lost their jobs and businesses are closing. Media reports slanted stories. The government is taking more and more control of the business sector; not just expanding on current regulations, but placing itself in the position of having authority to fire management of major corporations and now even shutting down those businesses that they believe cannot survive.

People who speak the truth are frequently persecuted and called liars. Politically correct seems to be a new way of life. There are many factors that have brought us to the condition we find ourselves. Some of these problems are self-inflicted wounds, but whatever the reason we find ourselves facing these challenges; we are here. This is darkness. Now what are we going to do about it?

If the previous paragraphs do not paint a picture of gross darkness, I don't know what does! BUT, no matter what is going on all around us, we have God, and we have His promises of a brighter future. It is apparent that the life described in His Word is a life not void of trouble, but instead a life that is full, and one in which those who embrace it will find themselves overcoming the troubles in life.

Isaiah 60 is overflowing with statements regarding the incredible life that we are to expect, and we are to expect this fine life even when others are falling prey to the darkness. This chapter in Isaiah covers what you may consider the smaller details of the quality life. Clothing and food, but also the weightier subjects of properties, business, our service to others, knowledge, protection, peace and yes…money; all are included.

Over and again, the Bible tells us to "fear not." As a matter of fact, "fear not" is in there 144 times. Fear is the opposite of faith, although it operates on the same principle. The only way to maintain a good attitude and keep yourself from falling headlong into fear is to keep your focus on the things God speaks of, good things and not the evil that is going on around you.

This is not just a matter of positive thinking. You might get some benefit from a positive attitude, but your long term benefits will come as your confidence in these promises grows. The words that come out of your mouth are from the overflow of your heart showing what you truly believe. Daily study will help ingrain these promises in your heart and mind so that when you are confronted with something contrary to what you were destined for, you stand firmly.

Think of this confidence as the roots of a sapling versus the roots of a twenty year old oak. Saplings have a main root and some very thin, fragile roots. When planting a sapling you need to brace it to keep it standing until the root system begins developing. Even then it is important to keep a close watch on it when weather turns ugly, and hard winds blow. An incident like this could cause your baby tree to uproot and without the protection of the soil; it would die.

In the case of this sapling, it needs to keep "plugged into" the soil, its source of nutrition. It is the same with you and the spirit within you. The same thing is needed for you to mature and be confident. You need to stay "plugged in" and then speak confidently.

As the tree matures, it is not that tap (main) root that holds it securely. But; instead, the roots that were very thin in the beginning spread out wide under the tree. They grow thicker and produce small thin roots that then spread out even wider and get thicker as they continue to be fed and nurtured. This thick base of roots holds that the tree firm even when storms blow.

Understanding that God planted you here and believing that God is in and on you is crucial to your ability to stand firm in hard times. No matter what darkness shows you, your confidence will hold you upright as the root of the tree so that storms in your life do not knock you over. Confidence in these promises gives you access to their fruit and speaking them reinforces the belief that you can have what they say. Every time you *"Say What?! ..."* it is like watering the roots of your confidence.

Creative power is in every word that you speak. There is not a word that comes from your mouth that does not have the power to change the situation or a person. Therefore, if you choose to speak negative words over your life and circumstance, over the people in your life; then you cannot be surprised when your situation gets worse. And if these negative words are spoken over a person, damage can be done to them that can take years for them to overcome.

So, today is the day for you to make a commitment to yourself that you will make the change from hurtful and sometimes hateful speech to uplifting speech. Change from complaining and muttering about circumstances and situations you encounter to placing a muzzle on those negative words.

Molding your world with speech is an interesting process. Heart, mind and speech are all involved. We have been programmed to believe certain things about ourselves and our world. Many of these beliefs place you in a position of looking at your life with "the glass is half empty" attitude. In order to change what you are saying, you will need to begin to acknowledge your feelings but not fall prey to doting on or meditating on them.

You may say that you are having faith for something great to happen for you, then counteract that good seed with complaining and murmuring about your job or the people you work or live. This is a challenge almost everyone faces and must guard against.

Most all of us have met a person in our lifetime that seemed entirely at peace. We marveled at their demeanor. We have never heard them speak a bad word about anyone else, even those whom we know had harmed them or attempted to harm them in some way. They were not a justifier of their actions, and yet people came on board with them and wanted to follow their star.

They seemed to be the most peacefully quiet person and yet they also wielded tremendous power in their circle.

This is a person who first knows who they are and are confident in it. When they speak, it is to lift up and motivate. They would, as said in one of my favorite films, "rather steps on their lips" than say one bad thing about another person.

It is because they know the power of their words. Not only the damage it could cause the other person in reputation or materially but also, clearly understanding the damage it would cause them both spiritually and physically. Most people like this have learned how to master their emotions and operate in a set of skills that are not the norm. This is walking in the light.

God is so good. In this verse, it says that "glory" is supposed to be seen on you. One of the definitions of glory is lavish outpouring. So even when the world around you seems to be going crazy, you can be sure that people will see you being provided for and not lacking anything.

In order to keep your mind and heart on track, you may have to stop watching the news every night. Continual reports of murders, corruption, financial markets falling, and every other ugliness cannot help but plant seeds of fear about how this might affect them and their families. These stories run over and over and over reinforcing fear, if you dwell on this long enough fear will take root.

Sometimes if I watch and read all the news daily it is difficult for me to keep my mind, heart and what comes out of my mouth in line with the picture that God has painted for me. I have gone through periods of time when I have chosen not to watch the news regularly. You may not be affected in this way, but if you are, please try this.

Right choices for you can keep you calm and collected while your friends and family are wringing their hands over crime in another city. People worry about things over which they have no control. This is not a prudent use of your time. When you choose to "fear not", it is far easier to maintain an attitude of victory. And that, my friend is light.

Start by assessing yourself. When I say assess, please do not attach a lot of guilt to your findings. The reason you are doing this is not to create more frustration but to "locate" yourself. This assessment will make you aware of needed adjustments to your mode of operation, and when made will create a more stable lifestyle. A stable lifestyle is peaceful.

When the opportunity presents itself, watch as closely as possible those people around you who operate in a peaceful calm. Even when it looks like things around them are in total confusion, they seem to take everything with ease. They roll with the ups and downs of life; coming out on the other side unscathed.

Conducting your own character studies of those around you can help you pick up pointers for your development. Observe remaining detached. If you are reactionary, overly sensitive and touchy, if everything in life cuts to the bone there is good reason to believe that you are not living as fully as you would like. You have the ability to change.

Setting boundaries is also an important exercise to keep the peace in your life. When you have inner peace, it is much easier to maintain a pleasant outlook. Even when something happens that may destroy the peace in others' lives, it is possible remain solid by assessing and choosing your response to the situation. Making responsible decisions, whether they are small day to day decisions or the major decisions of life, are easier if your mind is at rest.

Do you want people in your circle looking at you and asking themselves and others, "How are they able always to come out on top? How can they remain peaceful when the world is upside down? How have they maintained and been promoted in their jobs when companies are downsizing and closing? How are they living a better lifestyle financially in a recession?" You can begin to improve almost immediately. And then, continue to grow in this for the rest of your life.

If the gross darkness of our times is negatively effecting you, disturbing your peace, begin to ***"Say What?! ..."*** you want in your relationships, health, home and finances. Your life is your loudest testimony of God's goodness. God's lavish outpouring can be seen in your relationships, finances, and in your peaceful demeanor during a time in history when our world seems to be going crazy.

We can say, "It ain't over, 'til it is over." By your good example let others in your life know that they can experience lavish outpouring also. Show them the way. Speaking right words over your life (and theirs) will change things for the better.

THE CONFESSION

Masses of people come to my clear thinking, understanding and happiness; people of power, influence and position to the brilliancy of my appearance.

I am decked in gold and silver, my raiment is of fine linen and silk and embroidered work, I eat fine flour and honey and oil. I am exceedingly beautiful and prosper into a kingdom, and my renown (definite, appointed, purposed, lofty position marked by individuality, honor, authority and character) *goes forth among the nations, for my beauty is perfect* (complete) *through your splendor* (glory) *which you put upon me. THIS IS EZEKIAL 16:13, WHICH ACTUALLY SUPPORTS AND CONFIRMS ISAIAH 60:3. I USE IT MYSELF BASED ON WHAT I HAVE COME TO BELIEVE MY PURPOSE IS. Use it if you like or add another based on your assignment.*

CHAPTER 3

Come Gather 'Round!

Isaiah 60:3
And the Gentiles shall come to thy light, and kings to the brightness of thy rising.

Isaiah is a prophetic book in the Bible. It is broken up into three major sections. This book is in the heart of the third section. Prior to this chapter, there was a separation that had occurred between God and his people. It seems that they were seriously wondering after years of exile whether he would help them out of the dilemma they found themselves.

In Isaiah 59, God tells them that his hand is not so short that he cannot or will not help and that his hearing has not dulled to their cries for help. He reminds them that it is their own thoughts and actions that have created the separation. He lists the things that have separated them from him so that they could self-assess and gives them the opportunity to change.

Mid-way through the chapter they began to acknowledge that they were off course and living incorrectly. Deceived, deceiving and living a life full of wrong thinking leading to wrong doing. They even state that they feel blind at noonday when the sun is at its highest they cannot see clearly. They confess that they have done wrong and are in a place that no matter what they attempt, nothing is working out right.

Can you see any similarities to our current day conditions? The whole world seems to be in this position today. Being that this is a prophetic book, if we apply the advice given, we can see that we have a choice to turn from those things in our lives that are lending to the chaos.

Isaiah 59:20-21 states that a Redeemer will come to those who turn from their transgressions. "As for Me; this is My covenant with them, says the LORD: My Spirit that is upon you, and My words that I have put in your mouth shall not depart from your mouth, nor from the mouth of your offspring, nor from the mouth of your offspring's offspring, says the LORD, from now and forever." He states here that it is our part to continue to speak His words from now and forever. *"Say What?! ..."* His words!

But where do we start? Well, He begins in the very next sentence not only to sketch out, but fill in details of a glorious word picture of the life He had planned for us to live. Remember, when the Bible was originally written it was not broken up into chapter and verse as we see it today. So what is this next sentence? It is the first sentence of Isaiah 60; the very chapter that we are studying!

So let's get back to it. Gentiles is a word that not only means people outside of His people (meaning Jewish men and women), but also means masses of people. Christians were once considered Gentiles, but now we are in the family and heirs of the promises.

In your day to day life, you may be fortunate enough to work in an environment where all people think and believe just as you do. However, in the majority of workplaces the folks you work with are fairly diversified in belief systems. No matter their belief system many people are lonely, afraid, and cynical; they have been hurt by people and circumstances. They are in need of comfort, support, and wise counsel.

You may be the only light in your workplace, in some cases, the only light in a particular person's life. As you grow closer in your relationship to Him, you find those people are drawn to you. You may feel as though you have been magnetized. Those who are hurting may want to talk to you.

All of a sudden people who have previously not opened up to you may begin to do so. They may feel compelled to tell you their troubles and/or fears. They may be drawn to your sense of humor.

Your experiences in life have prepared you for the people that you are meant to help, for both your temporary assignments and your life purpose. Embrace the changes you have gone through and allow God to show you how to help others with what you have learned from your experiences.

Some of your most trying and embarrassing situations will help you to have compassion for the problems people bring to you. Things that you may want to keep hidden will help you connect on a basic level with people in trouble. They will see that you have not only survived, but risen above. This gives them hope.

I'd like to caution against the way you speak to folks and maybe especially folks in trouble. Be yourself, listen carefully to them and then speak wisely. I often wonder about how people expect others to connect with them when they are speaking church language; Christian-ese. The people we speak with day to day are not always church-goers, they may know nothing of the Bible or spiritual things.

Let me explain it this way. Have you ever tried to communicate with someone from a different country? It can be very frustrating trying to understand what they are saying to you. Well, if you are using Christian-ese and phrases that are common in the Christian community to talk to someone who does not understand your meaning, they may write you off as not understanding; if not downright weird. It could be very difficult to connect. If you don't connect with people, you can't help them.

Over the course of the years, the view of Christianity has become distorted. People in the church have not always done much to help the image. People often think of Christians as folk which are uptight, "holier than thou," and altogether too serious. Now you can't blame them in some cases. Many people have had experiences with the church that are less than desirable. They have not found the love and acceptance spoken about in the Bible. Help them find that love.

Just be yourself, your personal best. Being your "personal best" is an ongoing process. Build your character. If there are areas you want to change in your life, begin working on them. People can change; you are in a position to initiate the change that other people will notice and want to follow. Be reliable.

Care about the people in your circle. Reach out to them and let them know that you care. When you make a mistake admit to it. Now you notice I said, "when" not "if". You will have good days, and you will have bad days. Mistakes will be made, wrong decisions decided, and words spoken you wish you were able to take back.

Learn from these situations. There will come a time when you have the opportunity to respond to a similar situation; in a different manner. You will handle it with more finesse. You will also be able to use what you have learned to help someone else.

One of the most exciting things that you can experience is having people in higher positions ask for your opinion and expertise, and they will use that information to make their decision. "People of power, influence, and position" come to your "clear thinking, understanding, and happiness." These are the "kings" spoken of in this verse.

It is a difficult experience to describe. The first time this happened to me, I was in awe, but I have seen God's favor in similar situations happen time and time again. Expect the unexpected in this area of your life. God has placed a seed of greatness in you, and, as it grows, others may see the flower of greatness even before you do.

Proverbs 18:16 says, "A man's gift maketh room for him, and bringeth him before great men." The great thing is that you don't have to try to jockey for this position. What a wonderful thing this is, when you just keep busy doing the best you can do, and your skills and talents make you visible to others. There is no more need to clamor for recognition. What a stress reliever!

You may hear people speak of you in a way that places you above where you think you belong, or may be comfortable. Listen to what others say about you. They may label you a notch or two (or ten) above where you currently are. Accept this. Without fully understanding what they are doing, they, have caught a glimpse of the future; your future. They are sensing and speaking a promotion into your life.

This may be done in a joking fashion; however, I have also had this happen when someone in my life was angry or jealous. In one instance during a confrontation a person said that I was acting as a queen. If I am not mistaken they called me Queenie. The idea was that I was attempting to lord it over them, when, in fact, I was enforcing a boundary.

The comment was meant to insult me, but on reflection I decided that it was a sign of things to come. I chose not to be insulted. Instead, I chose to believe this as a confirmation of the word that tells me that I am "…the head and not the tail, above only and not beneath…" You see, this person was angry and felt threatened because a clear boundary had been crossed, and the consequences of their actions placed them in a position where they could suffer a loss.

When enforcing boundaries, those you confront may react in a number of ways. Name calling may be one of them. Remember, speaking the right things over and into your life has a lot to do with how you accept and process the information that comes to you.

If you notice, I placed Ezekiel 16:13 after Isaiah 60:3 because this verse confirms people being drawn into you because of "the brilliancy of your appearance." The glory (magnificent copiousness) of God, His light, was never meant to be hidden. People are drawn to and give favor to those who are brilliant, those who shine. You shine through outside appearance as well as your inner attributes.

Presenting yourself in the best light is a key. Many years ago it was important to dress for success. You can be assured that people respond better to those who spend that extra few minutes to be polished in their look, whether they are in a suit or blue jeans. I urge you to test this theory. The place doesn't matter. It could be a grocery store, your favorite sit down restaurant or traveling an airline. Press your clothing, clean or shine your shoes, make sure your hair is impeccable, dab on your favorite cologne, and ladies, freshen your makeup.

Then watch to see the added level of service and favor (even extraordinary service) that you receive because you look your best. You may not have a closet full of clothes. You may be starting out with only one suit or dress. Wear it freshly pressed, head held high, treating the people you meet with respect and look your brilliant best. It will pay dividends as people are drawn to you.

Remember that speaking without action will not produce the results you desire. Embrace this, your new found favor and ***"Say What?! ..."*** you desire to see in your life, taking the necessary steps to move in the direction of your dreams. Then, watch your life begin to change.

THE CONFESSION

I lift my eyes and see! Masses of people unite and come to me. My sons (the builders of my house) come from far and wide; my daughters are supported and built up and have assurance at my side.

CHAPTER 4

Support: Giving and Receiving It

Isaiah 60:4
Lift up thine eyes round about, and see: all they gather themselves together, they come to thee: thy sons shall come from far, and thy daughters shall be nursed at thy side.

People! Someone said, "you can't live with 'em, and you can't live without 'em." I tried to live without people for many years of my life and, frankly, it just doesn't work. Maybe you have too. Isolation is sought frequently in response to hurts experienced, and believing this will keep similar hurts from happening again.

Although some people hurt, betray and use others, there are those who want to get near you to show their belief in you, stand with and for you, and love you. People are at the center of nearly every disappointment but are also at the center of every joyous moment. What is a celebration if you have no one with which to share it?

Opening up to let someone know you is a risk, but one worth taking. We all have been hurt multitudes of times in our lives. Many of them happen because of a lack of boundaries, not realizing that you have the right to have them, and not knowing how to decide on which boundaries will serve you; and once decided, how to enforce them.

Having boundaries is both necessary and wise. Properly choosing and enforcing boundaries allows you to be more open with people than when you bend and sway to accommodate inappropriate behavior. This is only one step in opening up and allowing in the people you were meant to have in your life.

As you begin to allow people into your circle, your boundaries do not eliminate the possibility of being hurt; however, they minimize the magnitude of hurt because when a line is crossed it is addressed and resolved. This piece of wisdom may not be for everyone, but those of you who need this, please understand that moving past the emotional pain is a necessary step in moving into the place God has for you.

In order to accomplish anything of substance you will need people to participate in your life, and you will need to participate actively also. If I could make this change in my life, so can you. I believe in you.

Carrying forward with the major theme of Chapter Three, as you walk further into your dream, there will be more and more people who will come to you, wanting to be part of your life. Some will stay at a distance, utilizing your knowledge and wisdom as a mentoring tool. There will be people in your life to encourage you, and others will be there for you to build up and encourage.

In Hebrew, the word for sons means "builders of my house." People who help build your dream come in a variety of shapes and sizes, from all sorts of backgrounds. Keep your eyes open for them. Sometimes they are inconspicuous, and my belief is that there are some you may never know at all.

Even those who do not know that they are helping you are all a part of the fabric of your life or can be used by God to weave into the fabric. They and their actions are woven into the actions and deeds and words of others, and your responses and actions. There are also people who are working in your behalf. They see that "flower of greatness" within you and are pulling strings from the sidelines to help you along.

You may never know the number of things that have been done in your behalf behind the scenes, but whether you are aware or not, these things are happening all of the time. Those things others call coincidence are things God has placed into play through these "house" builders.

Remember: Romans 8:28 And we know that all things work together for good to them that love God, to them who are the called according to his purpose.

You are here "for such a time as this." You are here for a purpose. You are to lift up your eyes (look) round about and see (perceive, regard, view, have visions). See the people in your life and perceive why they are there. Are they in your world to help you or to be helped by you? It is for you to discern.

Psalm 75:6-7   For promotion cometh neither from the east, nor from the west, nor from the south. But God is the judge: he putteth down one, and setteth up another.

To me this indicates that typically you will not see a miraculous outpouring of cash falling from the sky; you usually will not find a satchel of hundred dollar bills under your porch in answer to your prayers. I am not saying that miracles without people are impossible. After all, "all things are possible to him who believes."

However, God often works what we call miracles through people. People who are receptive to that still small voice. Someone who sees a need and is willing to respond with necessary resources, no matter what they are; contacts, time or finances.

It is the favor of God that draws people into your business to purchase your goods and services. It is He who brings these "sons" to you from far and wide. Some may know you, and some may only have heard of you through advertising and word of mouth. God loves to surprise you with answers to problems or obstacles you do not expect.

"Daughters" are those that are drawn to you for protection, support, and nurturing. One definition says that this word also means "the apple of the eye." You have a responsibility to those placed in your life. Some of these will be men and women within your circle, and others will be outside that circle.

The people who fit in this "daughter" classification will be people who touch a particular chord in your heart. Love so often referred to in the Bible often shows itself in a "warm regard" felt for people in your circle. It is as if you can't help yourself; you just want to find something good to do for them. If a person is in your life, there is a reason, a purpose for their presence.

On the opposite end of the spectrum, some people will seem to be some of the greatest trials you have ever experienced. Sometimes you hold on and pray for them; sometimes you will need to let go and pray. Some you have an affinity with and desire to be a help in some way.

There are multitudes of people in the world who need help, masses who are in a bad situation. That nurturing part of us is pulled to "just do something" each time we see someone who is obviously in a dire straight. Every dime we have could be spent filling needs of those less fortunate if we are not prudent.

We are all required to help. We are called to help certain folks and causes, not every need we see. Others are called to other people and causes. The needs of the world will be met when everyone does their small part, heeding the call to help. Wisdom is to be used in the act of supporting described in this verse.

The way that I have done this is to pray before going into partnership with a ministry or other philanthropic organization. It is your responsibility to give, invest and spend money responsibly. Wisdom about each of these areas is necessary to do that. There will also be some spur of the moment giving when you see an immediate need, however, for me the same personal rule applies.

Through experience and prayer you will be able to discern which people you are to let into your life to support emotionally, spiritually and be a help financially; and those who you are not to let in. A whole book could be written on these principles alone. There are no coincidences, just pieces of the puzzle, parts of the plan.

Be honest with the folks in your life. It can be somewhat intimidating when you are open and honest. I have found myself in situations where I could have hidden my fears and faults. Feeling vulnerable is natural especially when you are interacting with someone you do not know well.

Logic would tell you that keeping your feelings to yourself is a better stance than being open. However, letting those who come to you for support, nurturing, and protection see that you are and have been fallible, vulnerable in a similar situation opens the door to better communication and fellowship.

Being vulnerable with people allows them to feel more assured than if you were to act as though you did not have issues or problems that you had overcome (or in some cases, still working on). Giving of yourself is one of the most valuable gifts you can bestow on any person. I am not saying that it is always prudent to wear your heart on your sleeve, continue to allow yourself to be guided by that inner voice.

As you continue to sow seeds of compassion and caring into the lives of others, you will see the circle close. A circle of strength occurs as you give yourself to others in support and then you are sent those who support you when you need it the most. This is another example of seed time and harvest time, what comes around goes around.

You will find that the more you believe in God's love for you, the more of these seeds you will want to plant. You will find more and more people depending on your support in one way, or another. In return, stronger people will be brought into your life for you to be supported and mentored.

Choose the people in your inner circle well. Those you allow "close in" need to qualify for that access. Letting someone in too soon can cost you dearly; emotionally, financially and spiritually. One vampire can suck the life out of you in no time at all.

Be kind to yourself and give relationships ample time and attention to grow. You do enormous good to a great number of people that are not in that inner circle, they particularly rely on your good judgment. Planting these seeds in the life of others is one way to walk in love. Plant your seeds. They will not be wasted.

THE CONFESSION

My eyes shine with joy, my heart thrills, for people from around the world flow to me, bringing me the wealth of many lands.

CHAPTER 5

Wealth from Many Lands

Isaiah 60:5
Then thou shalt see, and flow together, and thine heart shall fear, and be enlarged; because the abundance of the sea shall be converted unto thee, the forces of the Gentiles shall come unto thee.

For the longest time, I wondered about the seeming paradox of this confession statement. You might feel the same way. You might say, "after all I am just a small town person from the middle of the U.S.....or France, or England or India, or anywhere Plant Earth." You might be thinking about how little you deserve because even though you go to church you don't think you are measuring up to perfection.

How can you receive the wealth from the people of the world? We first need to remember to whom this was originally promised. It was God's people, people who had messed their lives up, more than once, and returned to Him. These were the Hebrews, our Jewish friends and brothers. And now as joint heirs we say we have messed up, returned to Him and can lay claim to these promises, as well.

The abundance (a noise, tumult, crowd, wealth, multitude, store, riches, multiply) of the sea speaks of a vast wealth. It is a wealth that his people probably could not wrap their brains around at first. After all, they had sunk into an ugly lifestyle. Now they are asked to open their eyes to the possibilities, awesome possibilities from a God who loves without measure. He is promising amazing things to those who are returning to Him. You may find yourself in a similar situation.

You stand in awe (your heart thrills) of these possibilities. As you begin to allow the hope and truth of these words sink into your mind and heart, more faith buds. The positive energy of hope and faith seeps in and takes up space once filled with negative thoughts and beliefs.

Negative thoughts and beliefs play out in our lives through negative words and actions which lead to depression and failure. And on the flip side of that coin, positive thoughts and beliefs play out in our lives through positive speech and actions which lead to success.

This verse clearly states that you will see (literally see with your own eyes, revere or be in awe) and flow together (sparkle, be cheerful, be lightened). It continues that you will fear (shaken, be in awe, excited, thrilled in today's language) and be enlarged (to broaden, make room for or to open wide). Why....because the abundance of the sea and forces of the Gentiles are coming to you.

Picture this, you have just purchased a new house and are having a housewarming party. People are bringing over dishes to pass, houseplants, new linens and other decorative items. Your parents come in, greeting you, giving you a card. You open the card and to your surprise it is just a card. Dad has already gone out to the goodies table and is preparing himself a little snack.

You try not to show your disappointment. So you walk out and give him a kiss saying, "Thanks Dad, I'm so glad you came." He gives you a hug, tells you he loves you and then slips a key into your hand. All of a sudden the disappointment is replaced with shaking and wonder, the key he has given you is not a new key, but one of a vehicle.

So, you make your way through the crowd to the front door and in your driveway is a moving truck. Running outside you grab your spouse. Finally after some wrestling, you pull the back door open, and the whole thing is packed with the new furniture that you had found while shopping with Mom. You dash back in the house, enlist all the guys to begin making room for this new abundance you have just been given. This is a picture of these words.

As in the example above the abundance (furniture) was converted unto you; it was transferred from one person to another. But we are talking about abundance from the creator of the Universe, not our earthly parents. His store of goods is the wealth of the world. Anything and everything you could imagine.

The sea is vast and covers approximately 70% of the face of the earth. Wealth unimaginable is there. And the forces (power, army, wealth, virtue, valor, strength, goods, riches, substance) of the Gentiles (amassing, a foreign nation, people) will come to you. It does not necessarily state how or when this will occur, but it states it will happen. This is his desire for your life.

Don't think this can happen for you? Stop and think of the things you see and/or hear about people of means being given; the best treatment, discounts, complimentary this and complimentary that, and gifts of clothing (just to have others see that they are wearing a certain designer brand).

I have seen interviews of celebrities in the entertainment and other industries speak of never carrying cash. One person mentioned that he hadn't purchased a meal at a restaurant in how long because he was always gifted his meals. You might be saying, "Come on Linda, I'm just an average Joe; I'm no celebrity." True, true! But, as God's children we live in His economy, not the world's; and in His economy we all have the same opportunities.

Perhaps an even more important and relevant example is the success you see in the Jewish community. Rabbi Daniel Lapin speaks of this, and the following few sentences are paraphrasing information he teaches about. Have you ever wondered why with the Jewish population only being approximately 2% of the U.S. population….why this percentage is not carried thru to the Forbes list of wealthiest people?

If this 2% multiplier were applied to the Forbes 400 list, we'd see this list having only 8 Jewish men and women on it. You might find it interesting that the number of Jewish folks on this list is between 60 and 100, depending on the year. And if we go down the list to lower income categories, you will find that there are twice as many Jews making $75,000 or more a year than non-Jews.

Now I don't know about you, but I could get used to that level of favor. Why would this be played out with this one segment of society? They have been taught principles of prosperity from a young age, they believe these blessings, and they believe that they are God's people. Being engrafted into this family, isn't it time we began to do the same?

So, is this a "disconnect" for us? One of the problems we have is that we tend to compare God's heart to the people we have experienced in our lives (and even to our own thoughts and feelings). People tend to be selfish and unreliable by nature. Even those who are not selfish, sometimes hold back, restraining themselves from giving.

When we were children, our parents most often have to teach us to share our stuff. I think we have all heard children say, "MINE." It seems to be a favorite statement, while clutching the prized object in their hands. We have been taught to give, but only if we have excess. Giving and giving lavishly, as God does, is a foreign concept to us. That is exactly what God wants to do for each and every one of us.

We may understand that our Creator owns everything, but we sometimes get caught up in the "how will that happen" thought process. When He transfers some of his stuff from one place or person to another, He can accomplish this more easily than you are able to transfer funds from one account to another at your bank. We all know that via computer technology is a pretty easy task these days. We may not know how it can be done, but rest assured He is not only able but willing and desires to do this for us.

We know that if He said it, it is so. You can be assured that the picture he has painted for us in this chapter is exactly what he desires for us. These word pictures show how he wants us to be presented before the people of the world. They depict how he wants others to see and interact with us.

We have been engrafted into his family, given the standing of a joint heir with Jesus, having joint possession of all that is his. We are favored. Do you have a difficult time wrapping your mind around these promises? If so, ask Him for help eliminating the stumbling block of unbelief that may be hindering your receiving.

"Say What?! ..." ever promises cover the area of your need, the ones that support the dream that has been placed in your heart and ***"Say What?! ..."*** often! He is telling us that there is wealth that he wants to transfer to us. Are you willing?

When you continue to speak these words, not just thinking about the promises but speaking them; your spirit hears you reciting God's desire and will for your life. These ideas and the love that backs them up will begin to build the faith you need to weather any storm that tries to knock you to your knees. You will stand and stand firmly.

To stand firm in hard times, you will need to have your beliefs and values settled in your heart. People are being asked to take sides like never before. There has been an attack against our way of life every bit as dangerous as the attack we suffered not too long ago in New York and Washington. It will continue to be a hard time throughout the world, more difficult than many of us have seen in our lives.

Personal responsibility, character and living each day strong in your beliefs can and will help to turn your life and this country around. You can become a beacon of hope to people in you sphere. You have an opportunity to make a difference like never before.

This is a time of renewed personal responsibility, time to help others. This is not as the government is attempting to do by taking from the prosperous to give to the multitudes who have become accustomed to being taken care of, but as it is written:

Proverbs 3:27 Withhold not good from them to whom it is due, when it is in the power of thine hand to do it.

Let this giving be out of our heart, from our overflow and with a deeply seated kindness that shows our countrymen and the world that we still are a nation of greatness. You were placed here for "such a time as this." Your experiences have trained you, sharpened you and made you into just the person needed at this moment. Do not let anything stop you from fulfilling your God given destiny.

I don't pretend to know everything there is to know about this verse or any of the verses for that matter. His word has so much depth, so many facets, which will take us an eternity to understand fully. As the years have passed and as I have gone through different stages in my development, this verse has taken on many different meanings for me. I have found that even if something seems uncomfortable to say, if it is His word, I have stuck with it and allowed it to work in my life. You can, too.

Athletes practice, musicians practice, speech-makers practice, doctors and lawyers practice. For how long? Until they get it right. By rehearsing God's word, you are practicing faith. As you continue to ***"Say What?! ..."*** to inspire yourself and shape your life; the words will become a part of who you are. You will grow into it.

You will begin to see those things that you have been speaking to take shape and be revealed in physical form little by little. Your dreams will become a reality if you do not give up. Your gifts, your talents and the abundance spoken of here are not just for your personal gain. He is telling you that fine things are a part of your inheritance, what he is expecting you to possess, and he gives to us so liberally in order that we will give liberally to others.

He wants to see our love overflow not only in kindness, but in outrageous giving. We have an exciting future ahead of us. Are you ready?

THE CONFESSION

My hollows are filled with excess gold and incense that covers me. *I am wrapped in a heavy robe of wealth, and, even though it is heavy, I am able to move more freely than ever before.* I am overwhelmed with being treated well and being done good to beyond the usual and proper limits. Exaggerated, unrestrained, and ornate resources are given to me. The hasty fruit of my seed, *my 1,000 fold,* harvest (Midian and Ephah) is complete and comes to me now.

CHAPTER 6

Hasty Fruit? That's Promising!

Isaiah 60:6

The multitude of camels shall cover thee, the dromedaries of Midian and Ephah; all they from Sheba shall come: they shall bring gold and incense; and they shall shew forth the praises of the LORD.

    I don't know about you, but I have a pretty vivid imagination! It is interesting to think of camels covering us. The first thing that comes to mind is an animal, A beast of burden; A BIG beast of burden! Obviously it was literally speaking of herds of animals covering a land, and we are translating this to a figurative picture. But, no matter the cartoon picture developed in my mind (being squished under the weight of this great beast); digging into the meaning of this word may be surprising, it was for me.

Although the actual definition of the word, gamal, means camel or a burden bearing animal; the root word for camels has quite a different meaning. It means; a payment to someone who has suffered a loss, to deal bountifully with, to recompense or repay or requite (return or make a repayment) and to bear ripe fruit. Most of us, if you have lived on this earth for very long fit into the category of people who have suffered a great loss. We didn't make it far in life without having some loss hit us, like a ton of bricks.

One of the most devastating losses ever experienced is in the knowing that you have not fulfilled your dreams. You know, developing into the person you dreamt of being when you were growing up. In the process of walking through life, something happens to a lot of people that makes them side-track, it prompts them to take a path named "settle." Settling is a detour in the road that robs you of the life promised in this Book.

Lack of self-confidence, life experiences, any number of thought processes could have derailed your dreams and making you think that they were no longer achievable or even that they were just the foolish thoughts of a child. This verse promises a recompense, a payment of what was lost; be it time, relationships, your golden profession and/or financial surplus.

"Will cover" means to plump up, to fill up hollows, to cover and conceal. Dromedaries are young camels. However, the root meaning for this word is to burst the womb, bear or make early fruit, to give the birthright, first fruits. Midian is one of Abraham's sons and his land, brawling, contentious, and the root means to rule, as if to judge or plead a cause. Ephah is a son of Midian, an Israelite, meaning obscurity as if from covering, darkness a sense of hiding.

This gold and incense comes, if we are to believe what we read, from some unusual sources. Some from people of a contentious nature (Midian), some from places covered up or hidden (Ephah) and some from some of the wealthiest of places in the world (Sheba). But no matter where it comes from or who it comes from; it will be fresh, full, and used to show forth the praises of the Lord.

Over the years, one of the things that I've seen in my mind's eye is what you see in italics (above). *I am wrapped in a heavy robe of wealth, and, even though it is heavy, I am able to move more freely than ever before.*

It is odd because you would think that this heavy robe would be made of velvet or satin, something very beautiful. But, when I see this, it reminds me of the insulation you see in heavy boots, you know, that half inch to three quarter inch thick gray woven material. It is not pretty, but oh, how it keeps your feet warm and safe from the cold!

This heavy robe of wealth is insulation against the ravages of poverty. The heaviness that is spoken of also denotes the responsibility that comes with the wealth. When you are given much, much is expected of you. Please do not shirk this responsibility! Responsibility is not a dirty word. You don't want to live your life just getting by, only going through the motions. Life is so much more than that.

Handling responsibility properly takes character. You begin to develop the character traits for this well before you are given much responsibility. Let's take a brief look at some things that will help to develop character that will support taking on responsibility. This is not something that is inherited.

Character is learned. It is something you train yourself to; something you learn. So if to this point you have had trouble in this area, do not be dismayed. Your change can begin today, right now. It starts out with an attitude of humility, a hunger for understanding and being teachable. You can learn so much in prayer and studying the Bible, but don't discount the life lessons encountered in your day to day interactions.

Relinquish your role as ruler of your life by choosing to submit to the leadership of Jesus, take to heart your Heavenly Father's precepts and listen to the leading of the Holy Spirit. There is a touchy area of the Bible that many people do not like to discuss. I used to be one of these people. It is the tithe.

I scoffed at a co-worker who tithed and offered. It was crazy! His wife stayed at home with their three children. I was baffled. Although I didn't know exactly what he made, being the numbers person I am I had a rough idea. How could they possibly make it, and why would he be so dedicated to giving that much money to his church? These were questions that were not answered for many years.

When you believe that He will provide for you and realize that you do not really have enough to make it, anyway; you change your tune from "I can't afford to tithe" to "I can't afford not to tithe."

Do you believe that when you tithe there is a protective covering over your finances? From personal experience, I have seen the way the other ninety percent seems to stretch when you have been faithful in returning the first ten percent in obedience.

Are you consistent? Can you be trusted to handle what you have with integrity? Do you consider before you spend? Some of you may have had no training in your families for this adjustment. Find someone, some books and a good counselor who can help guide you on your path to developing these skills. Then, take a leap of faith to take Him at the face value of these words.

People do things for me that even they are amazed at. Exaggerated, unrestrained, and ornate resources are given to me. This could come in the form of money, cars, transportation, accommodations, houses, jewelry, clothing, furniture, equipment, appliances, historical treasures, do-dads, and all other beautiful things; not just old hand-me-downs, but first class stuff.

Or this abundance could be someone's love, their teaching, one on one time, business advice, ideas? There is a plethora of intangible things that carry more weight than the material things. I like to run through this list at least a couple times a week to remind me to keep my eyes open to all the possibilities.

When visiting a hotel this year, I was given the choice of staying on the lower floor (in the room I'd paid for) or one that was a grade or two above. I think you know which one I chose. Recently I'd made a reservation for a four night stay at the hotel I like, but was informed that the last night would have to be spent elsewhere. I prayed about it and asked for help.

About a week after the original reservation, I called to see if things had changed. I was told that my reservation could be extended the additional night. Coincidence? Not in my book! I have also been given cemetery plots. I know this is a strange thing to feel grateful for, but I give thanks for every gift. By the way, if you are not aware, those two little pieces of property appraise out at $3,800.

Another example that stands out is having debts cancelled. There have been cash gifts when most needed, favorable circumstances in positions to increase pay, negotiated favorable vacation time, reconciled relationships, and many other signs of increase. New people in various positions have been brought into my life to replace friends and business connections that were lost, and with those connections come favor with investment opportunities.

I have been blessed to have these contacts placed in my life. These are meetings and people that I did not seek out. I understand that these are not coincidences, but instead gifts, divine connections. If I look carefully, I can trace some of these incidences back to seeds I have sown in the lives of other people. My being a business connection for a business owner or sales person, having cancelled debt owed to me by others, kindnesses that were given to strangers, etc. Keep your eyes open for extraordinary connections in your life.

The angels of God are gathering up the 1,000 fold harvest; good measure, pressed down, shaken together and running over; the 7 fold portion recompense from the thief;

the wealth of the wicked laid up for you; the silver as the dust and the raiment as the clay; your whole inheritance and bringing it to you as it is manifested through the words from your mouth. These are His words; this is His math. Pretty wild, huh? Wrap your mind around all that!

You control much of the process and what you are seeing in your physical life by the words that come out of your lips, the amount of seed you sow and your ability to believe God's math. He almost always is a multiplier not just an add-er. From my experience, if He ever subtracts or eliminates something from your life, you will thank him for it down the road. You will, eventually, see that the thing that was removed has been replaced by something of greater value.

What is God's math? And how does it work? I can tell you what he said about the first of those questions, but have no idea how it works. I can only say, it sure seems to be as he said. According to his math we are talking about; 30-, 60-, 100-fold what you have given. In this book, we talk about him making us and our seed 1000 times more (mentioned in Deuteronomy 1:11 and Isaiah 60:22). He has told us of the double portion and a 7-fold recompense from the thief. If you believe He is true to his word in other areas, how is it any different in this subject?

I have recently been given an expanded outlook on seed and how that eventually translates to harvest. Every element of your interaction with others can be seen as seed of sorts. Helping people, the attitude in which you do your job, going up and above by doing favors for people, extending kindness, giving clothing, food, information or money. Take any of these and follow them through to their natural end. That is your harvest.

Every time you choose to believe, build someone up, stand up for what is right, give to a worthy cause, bring a smile to a face, give a cup of water or a meal or a warm coat or rescue someone from horrendous circumstances, teach someone from your base of knowledge, live your life in love and integrity; these are seeds. Everything you see and hear…these are seeds in your life. Every word, every e-mail, every action and thought in every place you walk, drive, commute…stop and think about this…it is huge! Make a choice and *"Say What?!…"* Be consistent, and you will see results.

Remember: "The blessing (by implication, prosperity) of the Lord, he makes rich (to accumulate, enrich) and adds no sorrow (painful toil) to it." Proverbs 10:22

THE CONFESSION

All the flocks of men of mourning (Kedar) are gathered to me. The chiefs and strong support (rams) of increase, fruitfulness, and cheerfulness (Nebaioth) contribute to and serve me. They come with acceptance to Your altar.

CHAPTER 7

Money Ministry....Helping Those in Need

Isaiah 60:7

All the flocks of Kedar shall be gathered together unto thee, the rams of Nebaioth shall minister unto thee: they shall come up with acceptance on mine altar, and I will glorify the house of my glory.

  I have learned through my studies that just reading the Bible is not always enough. You get a deeper understanding of the scripture as you engross yourself in study of these writings. If you are still with us, you can see that we are studying each word. We are looking at the meaning of the word then digging into the root of that word to see if something could have been lost in translation.

I urge you to, when struck by a particular verse to take the time to read verses before and after so that you can discern the context it is used in, and then use your reference tools to research the meanings that may be hidden in what you are reading.

For instance flock means just that, but also means to migrate. Kedar is a place and also means dusky (either of the skin or tent), with the root word meaning to be ashy, dark colored or to mourn. This confession has been born of this style of study and often from the hidden meanings found in the root of the words used by the author.

People come into your life day to day that are "gathered together" to you to be influenced by the way you speak, the way you treat others, and the way you conduct yourself. They watch you sow seeds of kindness and love (hopefully not strife and division) and see the fruit of your actions and words manifest.

One of your strongest testimonies is what people see you do and in turn what they see in you. Don't get me wrong, verbal testimony has its place. However, I believe the strongest proof of that testimony is our lives, how we live it and what others see.

I am a loner by nature. To get out in a crowd, go to a party, or attend a function runs contrary to all that is comfortable and easy for me. If left entirely to my own devices, I would be done with business and quietly spend my time in my home (my refuge from the world) reading, studying, and enjoying my solitude.

With this seeming handicap, I get on well with people. As I develop relationships at work and church, there are times when I am forced to come out of that shell and do the work that I have been placed here to do. As a matter of fact, I would say if you were to see me in action in the workplace that you may not think that I have a side that is withdrawn.

Through the grace and favor God has given me; many changes have occurred in my personality allowing me to function well, developing new contacts, negotiating and of all things; small talk! Allowing people in, to understand who you are and how you operate is a risk, but one well rewarded as you see those around you develop because of your influence.

Let's look at each of the attributes of Nebiaoth, increase, fruitfulness, and cheerfulness. Increase is difficult in these times if you are looking to do this through the same avenues as your parents and grandparents. A regular job is prudent and wise choice as a starting point. However, it is no longer normal that you start with a company and stay there for 25-45 years and walk away with full retirement and benefits.

Many companies expect that their salaried employees work 45 hours for 40 hours of pay. Overtime is restricted and even denied by many companies, even when there is an overabundance of work to be done. Due to this, you cannot expect to be able to gain even a little by working overtime. Today most people are fortunate to have good insurance while with the company for which they work, but once retired these costs are left up to the individual.

People do not often stay in one company more than five years. The way the corporate structure is set up usually means that one of the best ways to increase your wage is to move to another company that will be able to use your experience and is willing to pay a higher price for it. This is a taxing way to increase and move up.

So, people are intrigued by and hold in awe the person who seems to increase before their eyes, especially knowing that there is a freeze on wage increases. Often this person is increasing because he/she has opened other avenues for this increase to enter their life.

Giving to others, wise investing, inventing new products or developing improvements on old products, or creative writing (either fiction or non-fiction pieces). You can open doors for increase by sowing seed as a pathway for the increase to enter your life. This increase gives glory to God (it makes Him look good to others) and hope to people who have been watching you.

Make no mistake! People do watch you. Although they may not know why, they are drawn into you as this happens. This increase comes not only through planting the seeds for harvest or increase in giving tithe and offerings, but is also manifested through the right words being spoken over your life.

Fruitfulness is about harvest. Harvest can be financial, but it can also be found in the area of relationships. So much can come through our treatment of others; it can be either good or bad. What kind of seeds are you willing to sow into the lives of others? Do you remember the old saying 'what goes around, comes around'? Some people have called it karma, but it had its roots in the parable of seed time and harvest.

If you have something going on in your life, some negative situation that is puzzling you; ask yourself if you sowed the seed for this "crop" to come up. Unfortunately, all of us can honestly admit that we have wronged someone at some point in our lives. Thank God we have the Blood of Jesus to restore to us a clean past.

It may take a great deal of self-control not to retaliate when the shoe is on the other foot, and you have been wronged. Your harvest can be hindered if you choose to get back at the person that is harming you. Most folks I know can say that they have been "despitefully used" at some point in their life. They may have stolen from you or spoken badly to others about you.

Take this to God. Lay it before Him and ask for direction. Ask that you be forgiven for anything you may have done to create this "crop." Forgiving the person who has wronged you is very important. Then pray for them.

This will seem foreign. And you may not feel like you mean it. Forgiveness is an act of will, not an emotion. When those feelings come back to haunt you, instead of picking it up again just say, "No! I have already forgiven them." Then, go on your way.

You have a huge say in what happens to you. To begin to turn around a bad situation, it will take a turn around in the things you allow your mind to dwell on and in turn, those things you have been saying and doing. If you are a praying person, and in these days praying is one of the wisest decisions you can make. Pray and ask for wisdom in the choices you make.

Cheerfulness is attitude. It is amazing how much difference your attitude toward others can make. Have you ever noticed the difference in how people around you act simply based on your mood? You go into the office one day, and life is good. People see that you are open and talkative.

The next day, you just do not feel right. Nothing is wrong, but there seems to be a cloud over you. How does this negative attitude affect the folks in your department? Well, my experience would speak a resounding, "YES." Folks want to leave you alone and are inhibited in their moves to discuss things with you.

Now you may say, "But, you don't know what they have done to me", "you don't know what I've been through", and this is true. I may not know your exact history, however, each person no matter how perfect their life may seem to look to you has been hurt, lied to, betrayed and in some fashion, been stolen from.

If you examine the feeling behind those statements, you will find that you are nursing a hurt. And why would you want to do that? Nursing has a two-fold meaning. It means to care for the sick or infirm, but it also means to nourish at the breast, to feed, to support or encourage an idea or feeling.

Wow! Which set of feelings do you want to feed and encourage? Forgiving and releasing a person who harmed you, asking God not only to help you get over the hurt, but also to change the heart of the other person. Or is it better to feed and encourage pain and bitterness continually giving it fuel to grown and eventually consume your every thought?

Feeding those negative feelings will eat away at you. Let me say that again. You! Not the other person. As a matter of fact; they may not even know the devastation going on inside of you. They are consumed and tied up in their own stuff and don't even know (or care) what holding onto this old hurt is doing to you.

In the grand scheme of things, this attitude of nursing hurts sets you up as a victim rather than you taking your place as a victor. Nursing old hurts can keep you from being a success with the life you were designed for and placed here to live.

What I'm getting at here is that you have a choice in how you act and are able to set the atmospheric thermostat in your life. You have a choice to remember all of the good that has happened to you in the last year, or you can concentrate on the negative that has contributed to this temporary funk.

This part of the daily confession tells you that cheerfulness contributes and serves you. It works for you. As you allow increase, fruitfulness and cheerfulness work for you, your attitude will be accepted as an offering to God. He appreciates and understands that none of these behaviors are easy for you to accomplish all the time.

In return for your sacrifice in consistency of character, you are promised that He will glorify (adorns, to go over the boughs) the house (family, human bodies) of His glory (honor, majesty, boast of, splendor, beautify, finery of garments and jewels). That family, that human body is you!

Things that may seem small at first glance, like cheerfulness, obviously mean much more in the overall scope of things. As you employ these attributes and work them, the reward is this; He will go over the top in adorning you with honor, He will boast of you; he will see that you are covered in finery of garments and jewelry. That's what He says.

People will be drawn into it all. They will come for what you have whether spiritual, emotional or financial help. You will have it to give. It is part of the promise. Remember that this is all a cause and effect scenario. He longed to have his people Israel return to him, just as he also longs for us now.

When either the Jewish people or we, as the engrafted family member, return to God; the promises of relationship, protection, wisdom, honor, health and provision were all returned to them.

So, return to Him. ***"Say What?! ..."*** he has said about you and see it come to pass.

THE CONFESSION

Who are those who are unnoticed or hard to discern? And who has a lively, exhilarating spirit? Who are lurking? Who are afraid or don't know how to step forward? Show them to me; help me to help them succeed.

CHAPTER 8

Discerning the Needs of Others

Isaiah 60:8

Who are these that fly as a cloud, and as the doves to their windows?

In the previous verse, we were just told that there would be people who would be coming to us. In my mind's eye, this verse is asking us to keep our eyes open for those who may not be a part of that flock described earlier. It appears that there are folks that may not be so readily apparent.

In this verse the word translated as fly, means to cover with wings or obscurity (a state of being indistinct or indefinite for lack of adequate illumination, unimportant standing), flee away. Cloud means an envelope, dense or dark. These are people that are hiding.

Think of this as what happens in the sky when the sun is shining then the clouds move in, obscuring the light of the sun. The sun becomes hidden from view. This happens to so many people. They were born with seeds of greatness in them; loves spilling out of every pore, and it is like you can see the light of God in their eyes. Over time without proper encouragement they are quashed down by hurtful remarks and events so they flee.

As a protective mechanism hiding emotionally, spiritually and physically seems easier than facing the challenges of life. This person may be overly serious, cynical and all business. They may not be aware that this is part of the cloud, the wall that they are hiding behind.

Unfortunately, this not only protects them from perceived or real threats, but also stifles their talents, skills and desire to fulfill their purpose. This wall isolates from constructive and life-giving relationships as well as from toxic ones. This wall can be very difficult to penetrate for the takers in life, but also the good people with something to offer those who are hiding. Somehow, somewhere within those abandoned dreams is the purpose that makes life so worth living.

The word dove means warmth and the root word means to effervesce (bubbly, showing a liveliness and exhilaration), by implication being in a state of intoxication, excitement, elation beyond sobriety. Window does not mean the window that you can clearly see through, but instead a lattice, or to lurk, lie in wait.

Even though these folks have placed themselves in hiding, every once in a while you will see and sense the light bubble up to the top. You will discern in them a moment of believing that they have more to offer, that they are here for more.
God has placed you in their life as an encourager; to spur them to attempt more, to strive for more, to come out into the light and live. I may be mistaken, but I think you will find if you get through the cloud they have covered themselves in, that this person is frustrated.

You may have already experienced this in your own life. Have you been hiding in one area or another of life? Was there a period when you believed you were here for one reason and instead submitted to living a life where you had settled for less? Have you ever feel friction between what could have been and what you are living?

The frustration is there because it is easy in this place to think that "what is" has to continue. If you have been able to come out of hiding yourself, part of your assignment could be to help them see that "what could have been" can be changed to "what can be." Encourage them to change and remind them that it is not over.

One of your greatest contributions is helping those around you who are in need. When you ask God, through the words of this part of the confession, He will begin to show you people and organizations that He has in mind for you to help in one way, or another.

You might be in someone's life to give them the benefit of your experience. Mentoring is a great way for you to help someone move quickly on their way, utilizing the benefit of your experience. Every element of your life experiences can be used to assist you in a teaching situation.

Rather than continuing to feel regret about some of the less desirable chapters in your life, look at them with eyes that see how they can benefit another person. These experiences may have been horrible when you were in the middle of the circumstance, but now with your instruction and/or guidance you can refer to those chapters and help someone else not experience the same thing.

Besides those horrible times, there were many other good times that you will also be able to use to benefit someone else. What about your experience in a job or some special skill or talent? Over the years, you have probably come up with short-cuts and easier methods to perform a task that will be useful to another person.

Take the time and assess what has gone on in your life. Whether good or bad, the total of what has gone on in your past has made you the person you are today. Who you are qualifies you to help someone else succeed.

Mentoring is a perfect way to pass along information. Sometimes you will be a personal mentor. Sometimes you will be mentoring someone in a business, sometimes in finance. Remember that you may be helping someone develop habits and character traits that will go with them for a lifetime.

This is a weighty responsibility. Whenever you are in the position of mentoring another, ask for help. Pray for the proper way to deliver your information. Be a good example to those around you.

In your interactions with others if you find that you have misspoken or that you were wrong in the information you passed along, speak up. The mentored person or group will need to see (and learn in the process) that, as a teacher, your information is not always complete, that you too are constantly learning, and you make mistakes.

Being open will gain you their respect and trust more readily than if you act as though you always have it all together. Let's face it, we all have room for improvement and all are prone to the same margin of error in our lives.

People will find it easier to connect with you once they see that you are not afraid to tell them you were wrong on some point and to ask for forgiveness when necessary. It also becomes a great example. People will see that it is okay to be open and truthful. They will appreciate candid communication and your relationships will be strengthened.

The point of this verse is that you will need to keep your eyes and hearts open for the ones you are to help. Each day you may have the opportunity to make a difference in someone's life. Pass along the skills, information, and lessons you have learned from your life experiences and the mentors that have come before you. Take that opportunity, sow that seed, and prepare yourself for a harvest.

There is nothing more rewarding than seeing someone you have taught becoming a success. Enjoy the process, open yourself up and share your most valuable gift. YOU!

THE CONFESSION

It is guaranteed that my islands, my coasts, and my desirable habitats earnestly expect me *(THEY ARE WAITING FOR ME TO CLAIM THEM; and I claim them now)*! My ships are coming in bringing my sons *(the builders of my house)* from afar, their silver and gold with them to satisfy every debt. The Holy one of Israel *(known around the world)* has glorified me *(you bring me forth also with silver and gold, and there is not one feeble person in my family; Psalm 105:37)*. You have given me this lavish outpouring (glory) in the eyes of all.

CHAPTER 9

Tarshish: To Satisfy Every Debt

Isaiah 60:9

Surely the isles shall wait for me, and the ships of Tarshish first, to bring thy sons from far, their silver and their gold with them, unto the name of the LORD thy God, and to the Holy One of Israel, because he hath glorified thee.

Beginning this verse is one of the best words in the Bible. Surely! It is a definitive statement meaning "YES", no doubt, infallible (unable to fail) and worthy of trust or confidence; you can take it to the bank! So this statement, the words written here are unable to fail as is our God who inspired the writing of them.

The word translated as isles means islands, coasts, and desirable habitats. A habitation is a place where a particular plant or animal grows. The root of this little word means to wish for, covet, greatly desire; something longed after.

When we hear the word wait, we think we have to stay in one place because you expect or hope that something will be happening. Well, that is a part of the definition but, it also means to bind together perhaps by twisting (to be entwined), to be ready for someone to take or to use.

If you think about it, when strands of thread or wire are entwined they are stronger than they were on their own. When two people are married, and their lives become entwined they are stronger together than they were when they were single.

These places where we were meant to grow, these pleasant, desirable, longed after places are somehow already bound to us, waiting expectantly, looking patiently for us to recognize them as ours and take root there to use them. This word tells us that they "surely will wait for me."

All too often we settle for jobs, places, people and things that are okay, mediocre (average or below average in quality, achievement or ability), when as you have come to see in this description of what God wants for us, His desire for us is His best. Are you in the right place? Are you achieving your best?

Everyone's life is not going to look, feel, and achieve alike. You might be a businessman, and your dream is to work out of your home so that you can have more time with your family. Well, your best is developing a successful home business. Another person's dream is to build something huge, so his best is to develop a global entity.

You may be an extraordinary shoemaker or a shoe designer. Your best may be to be a doctor who lends his life to treating the poor, or the research scientist developing a cure for a hated disease. Your dream may be to be a wife and mother. In that case, your best is making your home a haven for your family and developing your family well.

What is your dream? Are you a baker, politician, rancher, teacher, mechanic? Well, I think you can get my drift. The point is that your isle is waiting for you to locate "your thing" and working toward the desire of your heart.

But, first let's take a look at, "my ships are coming in." They are coming from a place called Tarshish. Tarshish was one of the wealthiest ports of the time. It was known as the region of the stone, a merchant vessel, a gem, beryl.

When I was growing up, I can't tell you how many times I heard "when our ship comes in." Well, this meant that there was no chance of us ever getting what we were asking for. You learn early that this was your loving parent's way to say "no" without saying "no." So, I decided to turn this around and use this phrase to my advantage. It fits so well.

The way I pictured this was as a fleet ships coming into to port for me with my sons (the builders of my house).

They are bringing with them silver and gold. This is working to glorify God because He has glorified me.

Every time you are glorified (enriched) by God, He is glorified (it makes him look good). This is in no way meant to be frivolous or disrespectful. But look at it this way, when we do well and are living well it is good P.R. for the kingdom of God. You are children of the King. If you walk around below your financial best, how can this bring glory to Him?

You are His representatives here on this earth. What ambassador do you see who is not wearing the best available clothing, riding in the nicest vehicles, being treated as the dignitaries they are? Which of these honorable representatives do you see not fulfilling the assignment they were given? If these ambassadors are not fulfilling their mission in a foreign country, they are brought home.

You need to take on the fullness of the glory that He wants to show you in your lifetime. There are multitudes of people who are leery about giving their hearts over to this unseen being; our God, whom we speak so loving about. They look at us and don't understand why we depend on Him. They may have heard that to be a Christian means you take a vow of poverty. And if you look at many Christians, it seems that poverty is a requisite; that's the way many of us live.

You and I both know that being a Christian does not exempt us from problems. However, if you dig in and begin to learn how to conduct your life according to the precepts laid out in the Bible, tough times won't keep you down. You will learn how to prosper in your character, your health, your relationships and your finances. You can learn how to live in shalom, wholeness that encompasses all of life's aspects.

You will begin to understand that placing your trust in this word will bring you profit. You will learn that any time we transact (do business) honorably, we are fulfilling God's first mandate to multiply and increase. Others will see and be curious as to the source of our success. Your life, your integrity, character and your financial well-being can prove to be your strongest testimony.

Wherever possible, I do my best to find confirming verses elsewhere in the Bible to give support to the Word that I am claiming. As a confirming verse, I added Psalm 105:37 "You bring me forth also with silver and gold, and there is not one feeble person in my family" to this part of the confession. This is talking about the exodus from Egypt.

This exodus happened in God's timing. Before the Israelites left, they were instructed to go to their captors and ask for silver and gold, and all of them walked out with no feeble people in any Hebrew family. This exodus was scheduled by God, his timing. The addition of this verse to the confession reminds me of the principle of proper timing each time I say it.

So this additional verse not only confirms statements about silver and gold coming to us, but it reinforces the timing mentioned in stating the order of events; first the ships of Tarshish, and then the isles wait.

One of the problems I have wrestled with over the years is getting ahead of the timing. I see something in my mind's eye, lay a plan out and get over-enthusiastic; jumping out ahead of proper timing. We spoke previously about letting peace rule these decisions, and when you jump ahead peace is not usually ruling, but adrenalin.

Wait for that peace and listen for your queue from God. He will let you know when your exodus time is near. When this happens, you will be increased and stronger. The exodus may be from a job. Maybe your exodus will be from a troubled situation where better opportunities will be on the other side.

You have to start somewhere and often when we start we haven't logged many successes. You may not have accomplished your goals yet, but if you continue to believe and take the necessary steps you will come to success. Do not let another person's skepticism hinder your progress.

I urge you to begin to see money and the transaction that helped place it in your pocket as a worthy. This is a moral and deliberate exchange that has helped not only both parties; but will also go on to serve or buy the goods and services of others. This is the stuff that America is made of. Free enterprise at its best!

Some of you may not feel comfortable driving around in a Rolls Royce, I understand that. I am not suggesting that everyone reading this is going to be a multi-millionaire (or however many zero's you want to add). But please aim higher than just enough for you and your family to live a mediocre life. Without proper excess, your ability to help hurting people will be severely limited.

Proper excess is essential. Some people wince at the idea of having more that the basics. There is controversy over this, but how can you help others if you don't have enough to care for your own needs? Is there anything that you would like to see for your immediate family that you are unable to provide for now? Do you own your home outright with no encumbrances?

Stop and think about this; it is a lesson taught to every Boy Scout in America. Be prepared. Being prepared is being ready and able to do something, made ready beforehand, and equipped with necessary resources.

If you are up to your ears in hock, owing everyone for everything you have (or think you have) you are not prepared to help anyone. Not your family or your neighbors or your favorite charity. I'm just sayin'. Proper excess will put you in the position to be of service.

Are you paying on a car note, credit card, have personal loans or a mortgage? How freeing it will be to be debt free! There may be someone in your family who needs your help with doctor bills, back taxes, education. It may be your assignment to make sure that your nieces and nephews go to college. That takes dough!

You may find that there is a family whose father, and husband, has been taken from them through sickness or war. Helping people through a tough time takes proper excess. Your local assembly may have a project that needs that extra cash influx. Were you called to help them?

Take the limits off God and allow Him to place the full extent of His glory (his enrichment) on you. There is no longer any need to wonder "I know God is capable of anything, but WILL He?" Read these words over and over until the meaning becomes part of you, until the words sink into your spirit, and you believe.

He responds to your faith, your belief that HE WILL do this for you! Be courageous and *"Say What ?! ..."* he will do, then begin to see it play out in your life.

THE CONFESSION

Foreigners' sons build my cities, obtaining more and more day by day. Presidents and kings send me aid (they minister to me, serve me). You have mercy on me, satisfying every debt (favor) through your grace.

You give me great and goodly cities that I built not (actual cities, apartment buildings, businesses, etc.), houses filled with all good things that I filled not (you bring me houses and all their good contents, even surprise hidden wealth), wells dug that I dug not (equity, an ongoing well-spring of supply), and vineyards and olive trees that I planted not (other peoples harvest, I will tend those orchards and vineyards, this may show up as property, stocks, bonds, commodities, notes, businesses and/or anything else you choose). Deuteronomy 6:10-11

CHAPTER 10

The Gift of Other Peoples Harvest

Isaiah 60:10

And the sons of strangers shall build up thy walls, and their kings shall minister unto thee: for in my wrath I smote thee, but in my favour have I had mercy on thee.

This verse is packed with information, so let's break this down. The first key word is sons. In an earlier verse, we saw that they are the builders of the family (or house), to build. Conversely, the word strangers means foreigners; this word abstractly indicates a heathen.

In essence, they are people outside of your family and inner circle, folks that are outside the group you hang around. They may be people you do not know at all or those you may have limited knowledge of or with whom you have little contact.

The word translated as build means just that; to build something, to obtain children. During this time in history children, the building blocks of the family were considered the true wealth, the true strength. They were spoken of as arrows in the quiver.

Fathers laid great stake in their children. Sons particularly for carrying on the family line, building and maintaining the lands. And through daughter's marriage, alliances were forged for added wealth and protection.

The word translated as build can also mean make, repair, set-up and surely. In the previous chapter, we discussed another important word, but it is worth repeating; this word is surely. It is defined as to depend or to be dependable; to be physically secure and unfailing. "Thy" means you or yours. Your walls!

And the word walls means; to join, a wall of protection, wall or walled. I chose the word cities to describe this picture because the established cities of this time were surrounded by walls of protection and in the larger cities these walls were thick and wide.

Our understanding is that some of these walls were so wide that they could contain horses, chariots and weapons up on top; within the walls of these cities were dwelling places and shops. Give this some thought. Read the words, this is not me saying this. It is God talking to you telling you what he has arranged for you.

This verse goes on to talk of kings, rulers, people in leadership and once again the word surely (pops up as part of the definition). It states that kings, these leaders will minister to, attend to (as menial, or of low status), contribute to or serve. But, who does it say they will serve? Thee – again folks – that's you! How can you not get excited about the prospect of the most unexpected of people contributing to and helping you in life?

Now a portion of a sentence dedicated to some serious words. When it speaks of the wrath (defined as splintered, chipped off, rage, strife) he is reminding us of the situation that his people were living as described in Isaiah 59. We spoke a little of this history earlier.

They were in awe that after their rebellion when they had given themselves to selfishness and doing things the way they wanted to do them; the God that they had turned their back on, once again was not only willing but desired to redeem them. He made it clear that he wanted to restore to them all that he had originally designed for them.

By turning their back on God and his ways, they ended up in a mess of their own making. In their own words, "...they conceive mischief and bring forth iniquity." They created their own living hell. The word translated as smote in this verse means to strike either literally or figuratively.

Most of us have found ourselves in a place where we have tried things our own way. We have begun to deal selfishly instead of being benevolent. We have lied instead of telling the truth. We stole something that was not ours to take. Or, we treated others in a manner that would offend us if it happened to us.

There may have been a time when you were just plainly mad at God, not understanding why the situation is as it is; knowing that an omnipotent God could make the changes to make everything just right and mad as a hornet that he has not done it. No matter what the situation is when you separate yourself from him there is an emptiness that no one but him can fill.

In that emptiness, it feels like you have been struck. If you have found yourself in this place of separation, don't remain out in the cold being battered by your own thoughts and negative feelings. Turn back toward him; with him you will once again find his favor and mercy.

In his favor (delight, desire, good pleasure, to be pleased with, specifically to satisfy a debt) he has mercy (to fondle...touch lightly and with affection, with brushing motions, to love, especially to have compassion upon, love, have pity, surely) on you. It is His delight, desire and good pleasure to love, touch you lightly with affection and be a sure thing for you in your life.

I do not want to pass over this statement "to satisfy a debt." If God's favor is delight, desire, good pleasure and to satisfy a debt, is there a reason more of us have not accepted this from him? I have made a commitment to him to choose to receive this gift.

We all know some people get things that they did not work for, but for the largest share of us, we associate having with working to have. What I like most about this verse is that it does not say that I am obligated to get any of this through my own devices.

We could not work enough overtime to pay for some of the extras in life. Fortunately, He is not asking you to work overtime. He is saying that because He is placing glory (enrichment) on you and your life, because you are His, He will see to it that other people around you will work, and you will profit. They will build for you.

I am not saying that there would be no work for us to do. Work was instituted early in our history. Adam and Eve had the job of tending the garden, etc. The mandate was given to be fruitful and multiply. We are to be productive, but it looks like some of the heavy lifting will be done by others.

On top of that, leaders; kings will minister to you. Minister means to serve. This is another uncommon promise from our uncommon God. I do not know how any of this manifests, but I do know that unless you know about it and receive it as your own, you may not ever see it.

I have seen small instances of this in my own life; one of the vice presidents of a company blessing me with a financial gift at Christmas time, favor for my department by the kings in our business. No matter what I have seen so far, my belief is that there is more, much more that I have yet to experience.

How He will arrange this, I do not know. I expect to see great things along these lines occur. I expect that leaders and those that I have seen as mentors will be sent to serve me. If you stop to think of it, these leaders have chosen to serve in the fact that they give their time and energy. Their voice and their writings pour into those of us who will receive the gifts of their wisdom and experiences.

Stop to think of the time it takes for an author and speaker to write a book, address an audience and record c.d. series or videos. Consider the wealth of information that they have gained throughout their lives. This is real wealth. I'm simply taking God at his word, and you can make this choice also.

Let's look at the word favor again; in His goodwill, acceptance, pleasure, satisfy and payoff. He has paid off every debt, satisfied the debt. You may have seen this as the gift of salvation, and, of course, that is true. This means that you are covered for your eternal life.

He does not want you to believe that you are good to go when you get to heaven, but have to struggle in a financial (health, emotional, relationship) bind for the time that you are here. Anyone who has ever been in a place where they are unable to meet their basic needs knows how alone and fear-filled life can be. This is not his best for you.

Conversely, you also know that money does not just rain down from the heavens. Well, not that I've seen anyway. So how will this happen for you? You may be able to get a sense of this in the next verse.

Here is the verse that compliments and supports this portion of the confession. Deuteronomy 6:10-11 states:

And it will be, when the Lord they God shall have brought thee into the land which he swore unto thy fathers, to Abraham, to Isaac, and to Jacob, to give thee great and goodly cities which thou built not, and houses filled with all good things which thou filled not, and wells dug that thou dug not, vineyards and olive trees which you planted not.

What a promise! The verses just before this one say this happens when you place value on his teachings and choose to walk as prescribed; studying, talking and teaching your children. Relationship with Him is critical. Talking to him and sitting quietly in order to hear his instruction. Of course, you have to know what his promises are to you in order to know what his desire is for your life.

The first thing to recognize is that there is a land (some particular place for you) which he swore. Swearing is to take an oath (to be complete, a declaration with a legal commitment to fulfill, fill to the full). He made this declaration to our forefathers to pass along to us. So when we are walking with Him, when we operate in faith trusting him for everything, he cannot and will not deny us.

This land includes cities; great and goodly cities. Great means older, mighty, noble, proud with the root meaning make large in various senses as in body, mind, estate or home, pride, excess. Goodly means beautiful, best, bountiful, large in amount or extent, attractive, of good quality and prosperous. Now these are cities you did not build.

And houses full (to be full, to fill, to overflow, furnish, gather, satisfy to the greatest degree, containing the largest amount possible). These houses are full of all good, the best and most beautiful things, that you filled not!! This is something that you did not accomplish yourself.

Wells are cisterns, fountains. These signify containers of water and in those times in the arid places that they were writing about the owners of wells were very wealthy. You see water gave life to not only the people but also crops and herds.

Typically wells and fountains in this day and time could be likened to an ongoing well-spring of financially prosperity. The root for wells is to examine, declare, explain, make plain. Could this also mean secrets being dug out, examined and revealed to descendants? Are these secrets revealed to us to make our way easier?

Vineyards (houses of vineyards and gardens) and olive trees have roots words meaning to be prominent and properly bright, planted, to strike, to fix, fasten. So, houses, gardens and prominence are given to us that we didn't have a hand in bringing to fruition.

It is almost more than you can wrap your mind around, isn't it? He loves you so much that these gifts are yours for the receiving.

Now that you do know about this, *"Say What?! ..."* he has promised by oath and choose to receive it now.

THE CONFESSION

My doors stay wide open around the clock to receive the wealth (the people, time, finances, and resources) of many lands. Leaders of the world cater to me.

CHAPTER 11

Who Left the Gate Open?

Isaiah 60:11

Therefore thy gates shall be open continually; they shall not be shut day nor night; that men may bring unto thee the forces of the Gentiles, and that their kings may be brought.

Therefore always gives a reason to go back and re-read what was just said. Listen to what the dictionary says: for that reason, consequently, because of that, on that ground, and to that end.

So, taken from the last thing said, "For in my favor I have had mercy on thee," consequently or because of that favor and mercy, our gates are open continually to receive from men the wealth of many lands. The sons of foreigners are building your walls of protection (your cities), and kings are serving, attending to and contributing to you.

Your gates signify an opening as a gate or a door, to split open, and in the root word we see the meaning to say to estimate or to think. And open literally means to open wide, unstop, loosen. This means that not only your physical gates or doors are open to receive but, also your mind, your ability to think and calculate, to dream and imagine, to build and grow will be thrown wide open.

Why? So that men will bring the forces (resources, army, wealth, virtue, valor, strength, good, riches, substance) of the Gentiles (heathen, nation, or people) to you. As before, their kings (royalty, people in leadership) will be brought (before you).

I have gone through many different phases over the years in which I have been making the confession. As my mind has been opened to the possibilities of life, I've seen these words come alive in a variety of situations. My suggestion is that you allow the words of this chapter and others of the Bible open your mind to all that is available to you; the protection, the support, the health and the love that is expressed throughout the pages.

Saying the verses that provide answers to your problems is a form of meditation. This form of meditation is very healthy. It sparks hope and feeds faith. Keep your heart open, and begin to see the different ways that this plays out in your life.

In a multi-level marketing situation, you might expect to see just the right contacts come into your life who will fill and strengthen your down line. In a business, the right financing sources, attorneys, and other support teams for your business may be recommended to you or they will solicit your business at just the right time.

As a housewife and mother you not only will find the sales and discounts that will allow you to stretch your budget, but also have enough surplus money to take advantage of the sales when they come up. Resources for innovative ways to train and engage your children so that their development is the very best it can be.

There is a right answer to every situation you confront in the pages of the Book. You can think them and may have some success, but your success will be sure when you begin to remember them aloud. Hearing yourself speak them builds an unshakeable faith for you to move forward in any of your endeavors.

"Forces" is a word for wealth. This wealth can come in the form of people, time, finances and other resources. All of these are a form of wealth. You may think that you need to do it all or that you can do it all yourself.

However, as you mature, it becomes more evident that you can't do it all on your own. You need to judge your strengths and weakness in order to build around those strengths and weaknesses a strong support system. It doesn't do you any good to surround yourself with others who have the same thoughts, strengths and actions.

If the only people you allow to inhabit your circle are those who agree with everything you say, never challenge you, or have all of the same efficiencies, abilities, and strengths as you have, what is their use in your life?

There is no way to progress toward fulfillment of your mission here on earth if your team is only strong in the areas you already possess strength. It would be like having a table top (your dream) being held up by one leg. It would be wobbly and tip over with the least bit of weight laid on its top. You will need people in your life who can take up the load of each corner of that table top. Then the dream can carry the weight of opposition and challenges that will come your way as you walk this out.

Assess your weaknesses and pray for God to bring to you the people He has intended to act as support in that area. Populate your circle with diverse talents and skills. Bring in people who are strong where you are weak and let them know that they are needed for their strengths.

People are one of the greatest commodities that God promises. And for heaven's sake and the sake of those you bring in; lead through edification not manipulation. Praise the good they do. Ask for their input when addressing challenges. And when correction is needed, do this with caring so that they know they are appreciated.

The response you get and the loyalty developed will be well worth it. Offer thanksgiving for their presence in your life. Pray for them and their continued success, and, by all means, show them your appreciation.

Some of the people that will be lead to us and guided to serve us are kings. The dictionary describes Kings as having preeminence in a particular category or group or field, a very wealthy or powerful businessman, a competitor who holds a preeminent position.

Now I don't know about you, but I will be delighted as I see this play out in my life. It is not an arrogant boast but a word of God to His people. You are one of His people and are choosing to claim this as your own.

Guard against needing to know the "how's and whys" of the manifestation. That is none of your business; it is His delight and joy to work for you and arrange meetings that you may never have believed possible. He will bring every contact that is needed to help you fulfill your destiny.

Things you could never do in a hundred years can be accomplished by God in a twinkling of an eye. No amount of human manipulations of people and events can produce the enduring results provided by your loving Father, God. Gratitude is essential. Remember where your blessing came from.

Part of the definition of forces is financial wealth. Most of you who seek out this material blessing are not looking to be wealthy to satisfy greed. As a matter of fact, it is probably not even money that you desire, but, what that money will allow you to do. You feel the need to do more and know that cash will allow you to do the works that are in your hearts to do.

You may have already figured out that sometimes I have been hard headed and tried to do many things my own way. Although my motives were good in the fact that I had the same desires to help family, friends and charities; more than once I pursued a path only for the financial results.

There are ample opportunities out there that will bring financial success. Most of those unless there is abuse of human rights involved are those where the transactions are morally sound. In essence, a person purchasing either services or goods from a supplier and both the buyer and seller are grateful for the other party and both profit some way by the transaction.

The venture I mention was not immoral, it was my misunderstanding of the spiritual side of the transaction that was lacking. My focus should have been on the benefit it brings to the other person. When your understanding is unclear, and you only do transactions for what you will receive as a benefit. A void is created; a little pit that can keep you from achieving at the level you want to succeed.

And, by the way, customers may stay away from you by the tens, hundreds or thousands if they feel you are only in it for your next sale. It is instead the process of helping others, being a service to make their lives better that will bring the wealth for your actions. God has set up a system where he has given us gifts and talents to serve others.

Many become side tracked by training in an area of expertise to make someone else (perhaps a parent or authority figure) happy. They may take a position, because it appears to be a stepping stone; not because they want a job, or are qualified. The decision seems financially right, only to find that they are unhappy at the end of the day. They have a hard time looking at themselves in the mirror over having to act on the job in a way that goes contrary to their moral compass.

Once on the wrong path, it is difficult to discern what the next right step will be. One reason is that when on the wrong path, confusion muddies the waters of you mind. Trying to figure out what path you need to take can be difficult in that we are so stirred we do not spend quiet time with God necessary to hear his direction.

If you have already embarked on a path that you find is not yours, it could be difficult to step away from a good wage and benefit package. You might feel that you have to stick it out until the "bitter end." But, if you wait to that end, you may find it bitter indeed.

It is okay to back up, rethink your current position and potentially make a change. Remember that even going in the wrong direction for a period, will bring learning opportunities. These may be learning how to act in a certain situation, how to treat or not to treat employees, learning new skills that you hadn't learned before.

A multitude of good can come out of even a bad situation. And, just because a season of time is difficult, doesn't mean that you have chosen incorrectly. Sometimes life feels more like a boot-camp than we would like. However, these are the times when we can grow and mature the most.

It is gaining victory over challenges and achieving that brings us emotional reward. Seeing something go from inspiration (an idea) to full completion is amazing. The reward comes from following the process to its natural end and in this success the money will follow. It is a by-product.

It was necessary to come to a place where I said "If it is not Your ultimate best for my life, then, I don't want it. If this is just another 'great idea', then don't let this come to pass. I open my heart and mind to You, and Your best for my life. Please show me what it is." When I did this and was sincere, things began to change for me.

When you verbally open your gates, and your faith builds, something begins to happen in the spiritual realm. Faith says, "Yes" when everything on the inside of you is yelling, "Not possible!" Remind yourself that this word says "Yes!" And, agree with it!

Remember: "I can do all things through Christ which strengtheneth (to empower, enable, increase in strength, a force, miraculous power) me." Philippians 4:13

THE CONFESSION

People and leaders who will not work for me will perish (wandering away and losing themselves), being utterly wasted.

CHAPTER 12

Are You Being Served?

Isaiah 60:12

For the nation and kingdom that will not serve thee shall perish; yea, those nations shall be utterly wasted.

We have already looked at the word translated as nation and know it means heathen, nation, or people. Kingdom means the estate or rule, a country or realm, something belonging to the king, king's dominion and the root says ascending to the throne. Serve means to work for, serve, labor, compel to do work.

When we put this all together we are being told that leaders; people in authority, who choose not to work in our behalf will perish (wander away, lose oneself or be utterly destroyed).

We need to keep in mind that this was a promise to His people who had turned from him and had messed things up badly. God's "hand was not shortened, that it could not save nor his ear heavy that it could not hear." In Chapter 60, one of those promises is that those who will not help or serve them will perish. As Christians, we are engrafted into these covenants. As joint heirs to these promises, this promise of protection is for us also.

Where do I start? This was the hardest of all the parts of this confession to say with the right motive. I understood this was part of God's protection for me; however, it seemed too harsh.

Now, I would presume that men would not have the same issue with this that women might have with these words. Men are typically brought up to guard, and protect. They have the mind of a warrior and draw clear lines in the sand.

I, on the other hand, ran through the gamut of thoughts and emotions. If I took this at face value, the thought of someone wandering and being wasted bothered me. And of course, if this were true then it appeared that there would be people who were going to end up not faring so well, if they treated me inappropriately.

I had always wanted someone to love me so much that they would guard me against the things that hurt me, but is this what I wanted? So many people had hurt me through betrayal, emotionally and even financially. There were times when I said these words, and they would seem to drip with venom.

Then guilt feelings would get the better of me. I'd repent. Other times, I would try to skip over this, and end up feeling like I was leaving important ground uncovered. There had to be some middle ground here. Through prayer, I understood that although there was a time for war, that any vengeance that took place was God's and not mine.

These words are God's, and He said them so we would know that He is there to watch our back. He said that people and nations would serve His children, and when they do not, He takes care of that. You don't have to do anything to make this happen. Leave it to Him, it is his concern.

There are many scriptures that confirm this throughout the Bible.

> Jer 20:11 But the LORD [is] with me as a mighty terrible one: therefore my persecutors shall stumble, and they shall not prevail: they shall be greatly ashamed; for they shall not prosper: [their] everlasting confusion shall never be forgotten

> Psa 33:10 The LORD bringeth the counsel of the heathen to nought: he maketh the devices of the people of none effect
> Psalm 13:12 The wicked plotteth against the just, and gnasheth upon him with his teeth.
> :13 The Lord shall laugh at him: for he seeth that his day is coming.

Our Father loves you like no love you can know here on earth. When people come against you with no cause, He feels every hurt intensely. He understands your questions of "Why?" or "How could this be?" He wants you to come to Him and ask for His wisdom in the matter.

When trouble comes, look at it, examine it, and decide what to do. Trouble can come because you are progressing toward your purpose and gaining ground, or from weed seeds you may have planted in your life through negative words, thoughts and deeds, or it can just be a part of your training. All trouble needs to be looked at from every direction.

Your enemy is not at all happy about your progress and is willing to bring almost anything into your life that will break your focus and keep you from doing the thing that you may need to do most. When you judge yourself and repent when you are in the wrong, you open doors for bad situations turning around. Remember, you have the opportunity to turn your life around by a change in the way that you think and speak.

As I was writing this book, there were people in my life telling lies about me. I have to say that I have prayed to be able to have the calm countenance that I presume Jesus had as He drew in the sand while the people brought him the adulterous woman. However, I have not reached this level of enlightenment yet.

I do not do well when people are lying about me, however, I am getting better in my response to this mode of attack. I feel the same as most people I know, when faced with this situation. I want to complain about the dirty deed and its perpetrator. I find myself often saying that "I can't believe that this happened", "What were they thinking?", or "What gives them the right?"

But, my best initial action is always to talk with my Father. As a matter of fact, during this time this was not the only obstacle I faced. I was also attacked in my health and finances. Without going into too much detail, there were a number of months when not a week went by that some trouble was knocking at my door.

It was necessary to examine each new and troubling event carefully to see if these were the weeds from seeds I had planted or a series of obstacles designed to keep me from the work needed to fulfill my purpose.

Admittedly, some of those circumstances were based in something that started with wrong words spoken, entertaining too many wrong thoughts or wrong action (or lack of action when something needed to be done), and they needed to be reversed with repentance. Repenting is simply to change one's mind for better.

It is not popular these days to label something as wrong. Many folks think, "everything is everything." The idea is that as long as it does not affect your conscience it is okay. But, people ignore the poking and prodding done by their conscience, when they don't want to hear it.

And, no matter what the social or political correct police tell you, there is a right and a wrong way to live. You know in your heart those things that are right and wrong. When you run contrary to that heart peace there will be outward evidence of that showing up in your life.

I'm sure you have heard the old saying, "Whether you say you can, or you say you can't, you are right." The words we speak come from the thoughts we have and how strongly these thoughts are imbedded in our hearts. First the thoughts come and are either dismissed or entertained. Once entertained, they are given voice. And, once thoughts are given voice, action soon follows.

Have you ever noticed that when you get mad and lose control, some pretty ugly things can pop out of your mouth? Cartoons show this internal battle as the little angel sitting on one shoulder and a devil sitting on the other battling it out to see which thought process is going to show up in your reaction to the current situation.

Life is a boot camp, so to speak. We are in training. And if you want to have a better life you are going to have to make some tough choices. You may very well have to turn your cheek when you are wronged. Changing how you think, speak and act will take discipline and practice.

Some of my hardest decisions were not to take action against someone when I had every ethical and moral right to do so. Somehow maintaining my peace, counting the emotional cost and weighing that against the financial cost, was the most important thing.

I have personally walked away from large amounts of money, taken a couple of huge financial hits to maintain my peace. Sometimes walking away is a better course of action than attempting to take a person to court to recover that which was lost through poor judgment.

If we relate this to seed time and harvest, this is becoming a twice sown seed. The first sowing is as a debt cancellation for the person that owed the money. The second sowing is a seed of peace, allowing the injured party (in this case, me) to move forward rather than being tied emotionally to the bitterness that comes from betrayal.

As these obstacles reveal themselves to you, seek Him. Review the kinds of seeds you have been planting with your words, thoughts, and actions. If you see that you have gotten off base in any area, repent and make the necessary adjustment.

If you have not shown gratitude for all that He has done for you, begin praising and thanking Him. If you believe that your temporary trouble is because you are on the right track, allow Him to show Himself strong in your behalf.

You cannot be held responsible for the harvest your perpetrators gather as a result of the random acts of unkindness done to you in your journey. You can pray for them; however, you cannot control people and the way they treat you. It is also good to consider that although you are favored this doesn't mean you will never experience trouble. It does, however, mean you will be able to walk through it and win.

Remember: "Be not deceived; God is not mocked: for whatsoever a man soweth, that shall he also reap." Galatians 6:7 Frequently this verse is used to beat up folks up, however, the truth in this word is not only if you sow bad or little seed you will reap on the negative side of the scale.

But if you continue sowing good seed you will reap a great harvest too. My guess is that you have sown far more good seeds than bad during your years on this earth....celebrate that and...focus on the good you have done and *"Say What?! ..."*

THE CONFESSION

The riches and honor (glory) of courage, understanding, feelings, wisdom, will, and intellect (Lebanon) come to me and are mine now. I am enduring, an instrument of war and of music, firm and straight, honest, happy, and prosperous all together. These attributes embellish the home of the Holy One. You make the place of my feet copious (rich).

CHAPTER 13

Character Traits – Elements of Success

Isaiah 60:13

The glory of Lebanon shall come unto thee, the fir tree, the pine tree, and the box together, to beautify the place of my sanctuary; and I will make the place of my feet glorious.

Here is another use of the word glory as an indication of abundance, riches, and honor. I love digging deep into the word. Glory means weight (in a good sense), splendor, copiousness, glorious, honor (able); and its root word means be heavy in the sense of numerous, rich, honorable, weighty, nobles, prevail, promote, be rich.   Richness, honor, abundance, and heaviness! Incredible!

In this portion of the confession, you name these attributes as your own. As in all things of God's word, you may not believe this about yourself yet. However, using your voice to bring these things into existence is what He created you to do. "Let the poor say I am rich; let the weak say I am strong." He used words to create everything you can see. He wants you to exercise your rights as His children and do the same.

At first glance, you may think that this was only talking about a beautiful building, rich woods and place of honor to the Lord. And of course they were talking about The (physical) Sanctuary. Looking a little deeper into the meanings of the words used in this verse, the meanings of the word Lebanon has rich and various facets.

Although Lebanon is a city, it has a personality that can be likened to a person. These personality and character aspects are spelled out as the meaning of the root word is uncovered.   Lebanon not only means white mountain but, also means heart. We are now considered the temple of the Lord.   And what you see listed in the confession are attributes of the heart in man.

Have you ever had a challenge in front of you that you have never before confronted? Perhaps it is talking in front of a group, requesting an audience with someone to present a business proposition, or even asking for the hand of your loved one. These things take courage. Stepping out on the dream that has been placed in your heart takes courage and a strong will.

Many of us have been brought up in a world where pursuing anything outside of the normal nine-to-five job is a rebellious act. These are heart matters. Strength of your convictions about your purpose and reliance on God to lead you will help you to overcome the obstacles in front of you.

In my case, when I first started talking about believing that my purpose was to be a philanthropist, there were people who thought I'd tipped over the edge of sanity. I was warned about greed and the love of money. The warning did not come from strangers, but instead from those I loved the most. This hurt as though I was been stabbed by a knife. You see, I understood that my desire was not only for my benefit.

Ideas about giving vary greatly. You may be like me. Rather than trying to talk me into giving, I had a habit of giving away even my last dollar. Part of my challenge has been discerning when not to give. If you have not been accustomed to giving, starting to do so can be intimidating (especially if things are tight financially).

Begin with the tithe. The tithe is 10% of your income. Giving this 10% as an act of obedience that requires faith. Somehow, acknowledging him financially indicates your level of trust in Him and his word. I do not know how it works but the remaining 90% stretches and has enabled me to do as much or more than if I were to have kept the full amount for myself.

Then give some extra. It will take courage to do this, but listen to your heart and give accordingly. Deciding when and how much to give should be based on good solid understanding. That understanding is outlined in the Bible.

There are whole books on giving but, here are a couple of nuggets on the subject. God will bring it back to you, as he says "good measure, pressed down, shaken together and running over." See what he can do with your faith.

Logic brought me to the conclusion that if there I had enough to help friends and family and/or fund ministries and foundations, then I would live a more lavish life than my ancestors. Proper excess over and beyond your basic needs will be used for various things; giving your children the best education, funding a project in your church or community, equipping your business with the best tools for trade, and yes; purchasing your choice of home, food, clothing, and cars.

This is what the Bible calls enjoying the fruit of your labor. In Ecclesiastes, it is written three times that man should eat and drink and enjoy the good of his labor. He does not say that you are obligated to give it all away. Some people, at a given time in their lives, felt called to this. But, by and large most folks are asked to be generous, not a martyr with their finances.

Have you ever walked into an exclusive club or stayed at a four or five star hotel? Have you noticed that many of the people whom frequent these places have a different air about them? Have you recognized that they seem to be vibrant and healthy at later stages of life?

When you can afford the best, regular health check-ups, whole nutritional foods, time to invest in exercise to have a healthy body, the body responds to the physical and emotional demands of life in a more efficient manner. You are able to do more and carry out whatever mission you have in life.

When you are just scraping by paycheck to paycheck, picking up all the overtime you can lay your hands on to have that little extra, it is more difficult to work into your schedule the proper nutrition and exercise needed to have excellent health. It is difficult to take your leisure time to rejuvenate your body, mind and spirit. Reaching for and walking in your dream can change that for you.

The pursuit of your dream will set you up for serendipitous meetings. When you are involved in something you are passionate about, time will fly; you will accomplish more, and you will be happy doing it. Open yourself up to dream and get direction on how to step into that dream, your purpose.

When you are walking out your dream and becoming all that you were designed to be, you will be an ornament. You will be one of the things beautifying this world. You will be excited about your life, and others will be able to see that in you. You may find that you are the pioneer of big dreams in your family.

This dream of yours will take all of the attributes mentioned in this part of the confession; understanding, will, wisdom, and intellect. As you speak these words over your life day by day, they begin to take root in your spirit and will change how you see yourself.

Hearing yourself speak these words rather than some of the negative things you have said about yourself under your breath or the tape that plays over and over in your mind begins to change your heart about who you are. But it also helps you see more of the heart of God.

To see Him as a loving father rather than a mean spirited authority figure in the sky, who is just waiting for you to screw up is what this book is about. When you change the images you see and believe on the inside, you will begin to see the outward manifestation of your words.

These attributes take some time to develop, so do not be disheartened if you do not immediately have all the courage, wisdom, and will you need to accomplish your dream. You may need to study things that you never thought you would give a second glance. Speaking the words about yourself and your dream will keep you headed in the right direction.

Confession of His word is prayer, one of the highest forms. You are saying those things spoken to you by your Father, and you are repeating them back to Him. Those of you who are parents know the thrill of having your child repeating the things that they have heard you say. You grin from ear to ear and just can't wait to tell anyone who will listen.

You want to do more for that child who is now showing the world not only by his looks, but also by his attitude and words, how much like you he is. How much more does your heavenly Father love to hear from his children those things He has promised? This is how he feels when he hears you defying the odds and speaking his word aloud. In a world that is in some phase of the perpetual life and death cycle, you are speaking life.

Your inner strength is built as you counter opposition with His word. The more you hear yourself speak these positive attributes into yourself, the more strongly they are established and the old (negative) attributes are forced to succumb and give way to the new and honorable.

You will find that as you change the way you see yourself, others will see this as an outward change in how you present yourself to the world. New people in your life may never know that you were once a person with other attitudes and attributes, seeing you as the person you have become.

These character traits are your formidable and undeniable elements of success. These traits show out in the definitions of the various woods mentioned in this verse. The glory (enrichment) of the fir (a lance, a weapon for war, or a musical instrument), the pine (enduring, a lasting tree, curvet...prance or caper), box (erect, be straight, be level, honest, happy and prosperous, guide, lead, relieve) was used to embellish God's church home. Seeing these deeper definitions described in these attributes would make anyone proud to call their own.

And the final sentence of this portion of the confession states that he makes the place of our feet glorious (rich). The word translated as feet means not only the physical appendages, but also your steps, your walk, to be able to endure, journey, possessions and time.

So, one more time he tells us he will make the place of your feet; where you walk, your journey, your possessions, your endurance and your time glorious. He will make all that you do both rich and honorable. ***"Say What?!**...**"*** these words decree for you and walk into your future.

THE CONFESSION

Those who looked down on and browbeat me come bending to me, and all who abhorred and provoked me bow down at the soles of my feet. They call me a guarded city of the Lord, perpetually confident, strong, and victorious. *You have made me so.*

CHAPTER 14

The Great Turn-Around

Isaiah 60:14

The sons also of them that afflicted thee shall come bending unto thee; and all they that despised thee shall bow themselves down at the soles of thy feet; and they shall call thee, the city of the LORD, The Zion of the Holy One of Israel.

Which one of us had not dreamt of the time when we could have an experience as the turnaround that Lot or Joseph experienced? The problem with that line of thought is that if you need that magnitude of a turnaround, you have either gotten yourself into or found yourself in some pretty dire straits.

Although your circumstances may never have gotten to the point of losing all of your family and belongings, most of you have experienced some period in your life where you wondered if you were ever going to come out. Would your life ever be normal again?

This can happen in different compartments of your life. It could be a separation or unwanted divorce; it could be a health issue that temporarily places you or threatens to take you permanently out of commission, and it could be a financial reversal. How were you ever going to survive, let alone make a comeback with people beating you up verbally, looking at and treating you as if you just did not measure up?

This happens a lot in a financial crisis. Adverse financial circumstances happen for a number of reasons. People can be downright irresponsible, especially if they have had no real training in how to handle money. Over the last several years business after business has down-sized or closed; putting people out of work.

In the old days, it was difficult during the depression when work wasn't available, but in those days most people were not over their head in debt like so many are in this time of history. Being head over heels in debt without savings to fall back on is a formula for disaster. Finding yourself as one of the down-sized this can place you upside-down for a while.

Then there is a financial crisis brought on by taking a risk on a business venture. Obviously before you went into the venture you did all the research you knew to do, your intent was to make a profitable business that could help your community, in turn bring prosperity to your family. If things go sideways in the venture, it can cause financial upheaval not only on the business side but also in your personal finances.

No matter the source a financial reversal, the emotions and the spiritual effect seem to be similar. It is embarrassing to find yourself in an upside-down situation. It is important for your own healing to own up to any responsibility that helped to create the situation. If you do not do this, you may continue in this trap rather than finding a way to dig out.

In our high tech world, everything seems to be tied into your credit score. Because it is so easy to research people online; obtaining insurance, buying a new/used car, renting an apartment, even many job applications are followed up by a full police and credit reports. These reports are used as a visual gauge of your integrity. In some cases, it is a proper gauge but in others extenuating circumstances have played a hand in the picture that is painted of you by them.

Many of the people who have picked up this book have been through some horrible financial situation. Although you may have never been through bankruptcy, you may have felt the pressure of financial difficulties more than one time. This is one of those times when taking a few steps back, and reassessing is helpful.

You may find that, for a season, you will choose to tighten your belt. Oh my goodness, during similar times I have done everything I could think of to bring balance back into my finances. I have moved to lower living expenses, clipped coupons, chosen not to have extras like cable/internet, cutting phone service to one line (eliminating a landline), not eating out; and taking on extra jobs so that I could increase the monthly amount paid on old debt.

It is possible to climb out of a bad situation. As creditors see that you are attempting to make things right their faith in you, their level of trust in doing business with you can be restored. No matter how stressful and humiliating a time like this can be, you will find that continuing to speak the words in this daily confession will help you to regain your emotional footing and rise above your current dilemma. It will build your hope and faith.

The strange thing about a time like this is that it is hard not to consider yourself in the same light as other people see you. It is easy to hide from creditors during this time. After all, they have the upper hand. The word translated afflict means to look down on, brow beat, depress and defile. It is normal to be attacked with negative thoughts and feelings.

You feel guilty about your credit scores. You are upset about making wrong decisions and not thinking ahead or handling your finances responsibly. You feel like the deadbeat that they continually infer that you are. A verse like this will remind you that there can be a time when the tables will be turned, and people who currently are not treating you well, will be vying for your business.

It will be as though they are in a contest to loan you money, carry your bank accounts, and fund your projects. Remember that, eventually, the shoe will be on the other foot if you do not give up. You will have what they want. Some of the people you needed to borrow finances from will come to you in this season of victory and need or want your help with a project they have.

They will, as this verse states, be bowing down, humbling themselves at the soles of your feet (so to speak). There are both satisfaction and hope that springs from this expectation when you are in a dark place. Hope will carry you through to this great turn around that He has planned for you, if you do not give up. I'm not making this up! It's in the book.

There is always something to be looked at when God repeats himself. In this one sentence, he talks of those who not only looked down on and browbeat you, but also those who despised you (scorned, abhorred and provoked). His promise is that they will bow themselves (humbly beseech) at the soles of your feet.

Usually he repeats himself when what he is saying could be passed over as too good to be true or something that you might miss. He wants you to know that your turnaround will come. When the turnaround occurs, people will not only treat you differently but will also talk about you with a different tone. Respect! You will appear in their eyes a marvel.

Some will know where you came from and will know that the only way that you were able to come out of the pit you were in was through divine intervention. They will call you the guarded city of the Lord. The root word for Zion means conspicuous, monumental pillar. How great will it be, knowing where you came from, when you are being called a pillar of your community? Cool huh?

While going through this tough time, your reliance on God will show through in your countenance, your actions. Keep in touch with Him minute by minute. The ones who watched you go through this will see that you may have been knocked down, but did not stay down. They will see your tenacity and perseverance. They will remember that you were perpetually confident (maybe not in your own strength, but His), strong (handling each step in the journey), and victorious (in the end).

You know in your heart and are not afraid to say that this did not happen in your own strength, but instead through your dependence on Him. You will once again see His ability to make you into the person he is speaking about here and giving you the victory He has promised. During a crisis time it is more important than ever to *"Say What?!..."*, then wait and see.

THE CONFESSION

Where I was destitute and odious (an enemy) so that no one wanted to hang around with me, You have now hidden me (from my enemies) and have made me advance (triumph) perpetually and given me joy without end.

CHAPTER 15

Victory Without End!

Isaiah 60:15

Whereas thou hast been forsaken and hated, so that no man went through thee, I will make thee an eternal excellency, a joy of many generations.

Whereas is an interesting word. It sets the stage, implying recognition of what the facts are and then is followed by a contradictory statement. And that is what happens here.

Although you were forsaken (refuse, left destitute) and hated (an enemy, odious); he will make you an eternal (properly hidden, concealed, for eternity, the idea of continual advancement, traveling toward a goal, victory) excellency (majesty, to be risen up, increase, an ornament) a joy (mirth and happiness) of many generations (without end).

Going through your hardest times, you feel pressure from every side. It helps to be reminded of others before you who have also felt the heat of the battle; both seen and unseen. Although your supporters will pray and stand by you, you know in your heart that they cannot carry the burden of this trial with you.

You may cry to your friends, discussing your situations, listening to their opinions and advice. The insights are often enlightening, and some help to lighten the load. However, when it comes down to it, you still go home by yourself and work this out through prayer and meditation.

During our lives, there will be a number of disappointments and even losses. It can be a financial reversal, as mentioned in earlier chapters that knocks you to your knees. It could be hurts experienced in childhood that were so severe that even your adulthood has been marred by their occurrence. It could be the loss of a loved one, unexpectedly or through a fatal illness. It could be losing a job or being passed over for a prized promotion.

Maybe your best friend has betrayed you with no visible signs of remorse. Maybe you have taken the risk of stepping out in a business venture or your third or fourth or seventh business venture to find that this one is not proving to be successful either. Your problem may be that you have made some horrible decisions that have caused your reputation to be diminished in the eyes of your family, neighbors or community.

And strangely, it could be that you are moving to a level higher than those in your old circle of friends. Trouble shows up because they are jealous or fearful of how this new level with affect their relationship with you, they are giving you the cold shoulder. Maybe just maybe, in your desire to gain wisdom and grow, you feel a loss in letting go of old beliefs and habits that have no place in your life any longer.

Again, many around you may move away from you out of fear and attempt to shelter themselves from hurt. I am not sure what your troubling situation is, but only your God is strong enough to be the one true support that you need.

During this time, you may feel utterly alone. Sometimes all that is familiar is jerked out from under you. Even your friends and family may not seem to understand. They have sympathy for you and yet cannot relate. Even when they can relate, sometimes you are so far into the situation that all you can think is, "No one has ever had it as bad as I do."

When faced with this treatment it hurts. A person telling untrue stories about you hurts. People betraying you in a personal or business or romantic relationship hurts. People who do not understand that you still are interested in having regular day to day conversations when you have a chronic illness or have recently lost a spouse. They may not know what to say to you, but this behavior still hurts. Having someone tell you that you do not have the necessary skills and experience for a position hurts.

This is the time talked about in this verse, a time of loneliness that evolves into a time of change. This verse is saying that when you go through a season when people turn their back on you, when they despise you, show you no respect, and have gone out of their way not to have any contact with you there is still hope for your future.

This is a time when a relationship with God, not just praying for your needs, going to Him as if He were a fast-food drive-thru, is important. The importance of having taken time or at least taking time now to learn His heart for you and your life becomes essential. He is the one who will not leave you on your own, but will make available the turnaround spoken of here.

It is bad when there are people in your life who are treating you with little or no respect, being hateful, or completely turning their backs on you. Unfortunately, when we are treated like this one of the natural responses is to begin to believe some of the "bad press." It is not altogether uncommon to begin to be a bit paranoid about others and their motives.

Self- loathing can happen. If not careful with your mouth, you can begin to beat yourself up about your part in your situation. You can speak horrible words against yourself; maybe not out in public, but behind closed doors or under your breath.

Instead of choosing to wallow in this sty of wretched thought and speech against yourself, disciplining your mouth to speak God inspired words over your life will help to bring your spirits up and lighten your mood. In a harsh season like this, you don't want to hear things like "times like these are used to test and refine you." Man that's the last thing you want to hear.

But, there is truth in it though. This is a time where He makes you more than what you know you are. In leaning on Him, relying on Him alone; your faith is made stronger. He proves Himself on your behalf over and over. The changes produced in you will be profound and life changing.

So, we know there will be those times when life does not give us its best. But what we see next should make you smile, a big Cheshire cat grin. "He will make you an eternal excellency, a joy of many generations."

The definition for the word eternal is concealed, the vanishing point, time out of mind, eternity; and the root word means veil, hide or a secret thing. Excellency is defined as arrogance, majesty, pomp, pride, swelling; to mount up, to rise, be majestic, increase, triumph; an ornament. Joy means delight, mirth; be bright, cheerful, glad.

I chose to craft the confession around these definitions by saying that we are hidden from these enemies of our peace who have so decidedly disrespected our achievements and our personhood. God is our protector. He can and will "hide you in plain sight" when required.

So, no matter how deserted and hated you may feel, even though you may be in a place where no one wants to hang around with you; this verse promises you will be "exulted in triumph" always (for an eternity).

Through these times, he gives you victory without end, makes you 'an ornament', raises you up and in the end gives you a sustained joy and happiness. Something you didn't have before the trouble showed up in your life.

Remember "And the LORD shall make thee the head, and not the tail; and thou shalt be above only, and thou shalt not be beneath; if that thou hearken unto the commandments of the LORD thy God." Deuteronomy 28:13

THE CONFESSION

Powerful kings and mighty people provide me with the choicest of their goods to satisfy my every need, and I know at last and really understand that You, the Lord, are my Savior and Redeemer, the Mighty One of Israel.

CHAPTER 16

Extraordinary Provision

Isaiah 60:16

Thou shalt also suck the milk of the Gentiles, and shalt suck the breast of kings: and thou shalt know that I the LORD am thy Saviour and thy Redeemer, the mighty One of Jacob.

In the last verse it speaks of him restoring your standing, bringing you happiness and joy unending. Now the idea is that you will also draw in the richness from outside sources and other people around you. This is repeated over and over in this chapter of the Bible. How many more times in the other chapters is this blessing of receiving wealth from other people (nations) mentioned?

I mentioned earlier that when God repeats Himself in a sentence that we need to sit up and take notice. Later it occurred to me that the whole Bible is a series of one statement being confirmed by another statement, and yet another and yet another.

It is my thought that He understands the amount of words, teachings and contrary information bombarding us every day of our lives. It is easy to see how trouble tries to take top billing in our thoughts and words. That is why it is so necessary for the multitude of reminders that we have a good God on our side; one that loves us and has success on his mind for us.

We need these repeated reminders to balance out and tip the scales in our favor. We want and need the scales weighted heavy on the side of success and victory to eliminate the effect of the negative influences we face daily.

Check this out. One of the meanings (in the dictionary) for the word translated suck, is to draw something in by or as if by a vacuum, and to attract by using an inexorable force or inducement. Inexorable means, not to be placated, or appeased or moved by entreaty; not capable of being swayed, or diverted from a course, unsusceptible to persuasion.

The words we speak are the inexorable force used to draw in and attract these products, goods of the nations and kings that God has promised us. I have chosen to say that these are the choicest of their goods because if I'm going to use inducement or force to draw something into myself, why would it be anything that was not of value, not the choicest of items? Not only that but, also because the root of milk means to be fat, the richest, the choice part, the finest!

If you were given a pass to go to one of the stores on Rodeo Drive in Beverly Hills and allowed one hour to pick up anything you wanted, would you just pick up the item with the smallest price tag? No! I think not! If you were given the ability, would you not pick up the choicest items you could find, especially if someone else were footing the bill?

Well, consider your free pass is the small amount of time it takes for you to speak right words about your situation and your desired future result....and *"Say What?! ..."* God has promised.

This verse tells us that we suck (drawing in by inexorable force) milk (the finest, the choicest, the richness) from Gentiles (those people, nations outside our circles) and the breast (signifying the nourishment and comfort found there) of kings (royalty, leaders).

I chose to use the term satisfy every need for a couple of reasons. One is due to the meaning of suck as nursing at a mother's breast. At this time of life for the infant, everything that is needed for survival and growth is found in the milk (whether through breastfeeding or the bottle) that is received. In all but the worst possible situation, mothers are at the ready with this milk.

Even in dysfunctional family units there is not only a responsibility to provide for the little one but, an overwhelming desire to do so. With a simple (and usually urgent sounding) request, this milk is provided and satisfies every need. The second reason for this choice of wording is that the term "Redeemer" means to buy back or purchase.

In essence, I see the time when we will be able to satisfy every need with the choicest of these goods. How great will that be? When times get hard hang onto your faith and hope through prayer, continued study and speaking well.

Results do not happen overnight; generally speaking. We are all in development, at one stage or another. Just as with every great success, some people will think that your success and accomplishment just happened in the twinkling of an eye. However, it takes time, faith, and patience to see your dreams come true.

If you speak of how bad things are all of the time, consistently take on the negative information that you hear and repeat it with your mouth, you should expect to see these things begin to manifest in your life. Make yourself awarer of the way you speak.

It is bad enough that much of the input you hear on your job, the daily news, television shows and perhaps even in your family unit has negative, defeatist tones. If you do not take the time each day to say positive, life-giving words over yourself, you may never hear any.

I do my confessions while traveling in the car each day. It is so worthwhile to establish a platform for my day that consists of life giving thoughts and words. On the days I have not taken the time to reinforce my life with words of power, there has been a noticeable difference in how I respond to the day-to-day issues that arise.

The more you speak these words or words like them, the more you will feel the faith within yourself build. Ask the Holy Spirit to touch you each time you are heading in the wrong wording direction.

And why has this been made available to you? Why will He do this? So that you will know (ascertain by seeing, acknowledge, discover, comprehend and declare) that He is the Lord your Savior (the one who has made you free and gives you victory) your Redeemer (He bought you back, avenged you; giving you victory over the one who recently defeated you; revenge for a perceived wrong), the Mighty one of Jacob.

He is declaring and decreeing this transfer of wealth to you. He wants you to see and experience it. He wants you to know without a doubt where it came from and spread the word to others of His goodness. The best way to express your gratitude is to *"Say What?! ..."* Not only for what you believe He will do, but what He has already done.

THE CONFESSION

You exchange my brass for gold, my iron for silver, my wood for brass, my stones for iron (all of my resources are turned to silver and gold, spendable wealth). Peace and righteousness are my taskmasters.

CHAPTER 17

No Matter How Small, God Will Use It...

Isaiah 60:17

For brass I will bring gold, and for iron I will bring silver, and for wood brass, and for stones iron: I will also make thy officers peace, and thine exactors righteousness.

This is so great! The root meaning of brass is prognosticate to ***"Say What?! ..."*** you think will happen in the future, make a prediction, tell about in advance, and diligently observe. He will bring gold (fair weather, shimmer, gold) from brass (you speaking what you think will come to pass).

And for iron (cutting tools, to pierce, holes) he will bring silver (money, the price, desire, long for) and for wood (firmness, to fasten and make firm, close) brass. And for stones (to build, obtain, children) he will bring iron.

He will make your officers (an official visitation, by analogy to oversee) peace (safe, well, happy friendly, welfare, health prosperity, restoration, restitution) and your exactors (drive, a debtor, by implication to tax, harass, tyrannize, distress, taskmaster) righteousness (rightness, justice, virtue, prosperity).

Every time I would say one of the verses in this confession, there seemed to be a kaleidoscope of thoughts operating in my mind. Different colors, different pictures as the seasons in my life changed. Above anything else, I have always seen this verse reminding me that everything is a process, and in the end, He brings every one of the original resources that I have to silver and gold.

As with so much in the Bible everything seems to be circular. Brass to gold, iron to silver, wood to brass and stones to iron. This verse takes what seem to be the least valuable raw material; wood and stones and turns them to the most valuable commodity. So it is with our personal resources and our experience. Even your harshest experiences can become the source of the most valuable information you have to offer to another in need.

Many of us grew up in a world where we are told that only those with contacts or money can make it. Our imaginations were smothered by circumstances and words that told us not to get our hopes up too high. We lived our lives with unfulfilled dreams and aspirations. By the time you were out of school and living in the real world, your hope for more than the reliable nine-to-five job was diminished, maybe non-existent.

The thought of doing something that was out of the mainstream was not supported by those closest to you, your own thoughts at times were your worst enemy. If someone else didn't do it your fear of the unknown probably shot down any idea out of ordinary.

The good news is that He promises us more. You do not need to be tied to the regular work world if that is not where you are assigned. With nothing more than your ideas and thoughts, no other material resources, He can guide you into success. Stop and think about it.

Every great invention, wonderful story, or handy-dandy tool began as nothing more than a thought or an idea. When you speak God given words, confessions, affirmations or personal prophesies, hope is renewed.

I am currently working on a couple of projects that require resources that I have not laid my hands on yet. But as I move forward, the resources are being introduced in the form of people and acceptance of these projects. So, I am anticipating that when I need something, whatever the resource will appear.

Of course, that means that I will need to remain open to unusual events and meetings. Much of the help you need to fulfill your dream will be obtained through people you meet, too. Don't discount the power of being aware of what other would call serendipitous moments. In God's world, there is no such thing as coincidence.

He exchanges our wood (to shut) for brass. One root meaning for brass is to learn by experience. So, we go from being shut to being open to and learning by experience. The more you affirm these verses in your life, your mind and heart open to the possibility of this word becoming reality for you.

Your dreams are reawakened. The creative side that may have been asleep for years begins to stir new ideas, new hopes come alive. As the mind begins to work and belief in your heart overwhelms you, you begin to talk (prognosticate) about these dreams and visions.

Another meaning for wood is firmness. Out of a firm heart you speak what you see in your heart and minds' eye. You *"Say What?! ..."* Matthew 12:34; states, "out of the abundance of the heart, the mouth speaks."

He exchanges our stones (to build, firmness; from the root established) for iron (strength, material for furniture, utensils, implements). This tells us that He takes you from strength to strength, building one experience and skill on another.

With each new accomplishment (experience), He makes you more complete and stronger. Each time you make the right move this experience helps you see that it is, indeed, one more step to the goal. When you make a mistake, and you will, don't beat yourself up too bad.

People who accomplish much in life make mistakes. When this happens, take responsibility and a little time to review the choice. What and why didn't this work? File your findings away in the "Do Not Do Again" folder.

Make whatever adjustment you need to make, and then move forward. Do not despise your small beginnings; they are helping you build a foundation for success. Job 8:7 states, "Though thy beginning was small, yet thy latter end should greatly increase." Believe that and keep building one small thing on the next. Now I'm not suggesting that you immediately leave your nine-to-five job to follow your dreams.

There is such a thing as balance and good sense. God is practical above all else. You will know when the time is right. Take it from me and my experience, leaving a position before the right time can place you in an unnecessary wilderness experience, one that can carry with it more pain than was ever intended for you by your maker.

Bad timing can create undo struggle, a set-back or failure; even if God gave you the idea. Timing is defined as a selection or the ability to select for maximum effect the precise moment for beginning or doing something.

When you place yourself ahead of the proper time, all of the elements of success in that venture have not been set in their proper place. Divine appointments are not in place. Resources (people, finances, even time) are not in place. Doing the right thing at the wrong time becomes a mess. Seek advice. Pray for guidance.

Respond to temptation with firm faith and patience. As you weigh your next move, you will have more insight as to when and what to do next. When you are doing the right thing at the right time, you have peace. It may seem that what you are doing is going against the grain. However, when you are doing the thing that is right for you, there will be a tranquility and feeling of safety; a quiet knowing.

There are many opportunities out there ready and available to enlist you. It is easy to get caught up in the moment when someone is presenting an opportunity for a new business or real estate venture or how to make money in the stock market. Infomercials flood late night and early morning television. Claims of being able to make a million dollars overnight abound.

Be careful not to fall into the trap that many of these lay for unsuspecting folks. Those ads are played late at night and are geared to excite the emotions of those disgruntled with their life's status quo. Be careful, especially when you are not happy with your current work environment. You can be especially vulnerable at these times.

This is when diligent observation (brass) can serve you if you wait. Research, research, research! Do not make the mistake of making a decision while you are all excited or moved emotionally about some of the inflated claims being made. Proper motivation is important in the decision making process.

If you are grasping at straws with your motivation being lack (financial or otherwise), your success level may be less than you would like. What many of the people who are promoting these opportunities are not telling you is that there is a lot of work that needs to be done when you have your own business. There's money to be invested, time to learn the process, setting up and working your plan; and diligence, truckloads and truckloads of diligence.

No matter the opportunity there is a process to reach success and it does not happen overnight. When you are in your own business, there are a lot of No's. You are hit with rejection over and over when you are trying to make it on your own. You need to know that this is the right path for you before you jump in with both feet. With the right support, you can make it.

So how do you know the difference between a scam and the "real deal" for you? The next part of this verse helps us to understand this. I will make your officers (overseers, to visit, want) peace (well, safe, happy, health, prosperity, welfare, rest). This is an internal thing, that still small voice being an overseer for each situation every day; that overseer is peace.

You know what it is. It has a physical and emotional feel. Peace speaks, centering upon a sense of contentment, a sense of well-being. If all you feel is adrenaline that is not peace. Advertisers depend on your prompt reaction to their cleverly formed sentences and testimonials. Advertisers depend on your adrenaline rush combined with desire to fill an emotional need.

Even if you do not have an immediate need, they know how to create them. Choose to wait and allow peace to guide your movements. Make your exactors (to drive, harass, taskmaster; those things that drive your thought and activities) righteousness (rightness, justice, moral virtue, make right).

This sentence reminds you that you are to make your decisions based on a moral compass. Is this the right thing to do? If it is you will have a sense of peace when the decision is made.

John 14:27 (KJV) Peace I leave with you, my peace I give unto you: not as the world giveth, give I unto you. Let not your heart be troubled, neither let it be afraid.

THE CONFESSION

Violence has disappeared from my land—
wasting and destruction from my borders.
My walls are salvation and my gates praise.

CHAPTER 18

Peace At Last!

Isaiah 60:18

Violence shall no more be heard in thy land, wasting nor destruction within thy borders; but thou shalt call thy walls Salvation, and thy gates Praise.

This was one of the verses originally brought to my attention. If you can picture this, I had quit a good contract position (before the proper timing). Another opportunity had presented itself with some fairly good claims at success and of course, the promise of corresponding prosperity. Early results in the business had been good.

I was no longer making money in both the contract position and this other opportunity. Shortly after this change, that financial spring went from full flow to a trickle, and continued from trickle to drip. This financial wasting continued until I thought I was past the point of financial redemption. This verse came to me as a breath of fresh air, one I needed desperately.

Financial lack is a form of violence (wrong or unjust gain, damage, injustice, oppression). If you have ever been at the point of financial destruction, you know that you feel like you are not getting enough air. It is a form of suffocation that is difficult to describe.

I grabbed onto the hope that sprang from these words. You need to understand that I was in a wilderness experience as a result of my wrong decisions (a horrible bondage). It became a bondage or oppression to me because I would not (at this point) admit that I was not in the right place. I suffered longer than needed because I would not admit that I had been wrong.

Hint: If you are hiding, avoiding people, not letting those closest to you know what you have planned and are only relying on your own counsel, you may be on the wrong track. You may be in the process of committing sabotage against your own future. Usually there will be excitement in this move, but no peace.

There may be the thrill of stepping out, but this move may be in presumption (that God will support you no matter what you do or what you have planned), not a real act of faith. This is where patience comes into play. It is hard to wait when you think you are ready. Waiting for heart peace will be well worth it.

You were not placed here on this earth to fail, but instead to succeed. One of the aspects of God that I am most grateful for is that if you zig when you should have zagged, He doesn't hold it against you as long as you get back on track. If you fall, you've not failed unless you choose to stay down.

To get back on track, He gives you hints through His word, friends, family, mentors, and counselors. In this case, my hints came from a series of verses from the same chapter of the Bible. This gave me hope (and the daily confession that this book is all about).

Poverty and business failure are cruel. In these situations, creditors treat you violently. Your part in this is often not taking proper responsibility for your decisions and actions. You may not have been a person who has had financial problems; there may be issues in other areas of your life.

Most of you have suffered some cruelty and/or violence in your life. In some area of your life there has been a time of wasting, ruin and devastation. No matter what your particular situation, draw comfort from the truth of this verse.

Violence here means wrong, unjust gain, oppression, violence against, or maltreat. So violence and all it means will no longer be heard (declared, perceived, reported or witnessed) in your land (your life), wasting (devastation, robbery) nor destruction (ruin, breaking in pieces, hurt) within your borders. Can you see why this inspires so much hope; an earnest expectation?

To think that there is a time set aside when there is no more oppression, a time when no negative deeds or suffering will or can be reported about you or anything within your borders (your area of influence). This is a promise to God's people, a promise for this life in this earth, not a promise reserved for our time in heaven.

Your walls are salvation. Salvation means to be liberated, victorious and prosperous. As you follow the direction toward your purpose, you will see each of these aspects developing in your life. Your purpose being fulfilled brings a liberating feeling.

Some people call this bliss. Others find that when they are flowing in what they were meant to do, they lose track of time. Their purpose energizes them rather than tiring them out. They are alive!

When you are in your zone, you see more victory than you do defeats. And even when something pops up on the scene that could be considered negative you can look at it differently and will find a way to turn those lemons into lemonade.

You will notice that events in your life flow. You will see people paving the way for you, and usually, when you are smack-dab in the middle of what you were meant to do, prosperity follows.

Your gates, your entrance (opening, and from the root word…your thinking) into all of this is through praise, thanksgiving. Praise means to boast, rave even to the point of being clamorously foolish, and to celebrate. Go for it! When you are in a bad situation, you need to be thankful, even for the little things. Even in the bad times there are a multitude of things for which to show gratitude.

When you are in a good place, you need to remember always to be thankful. I am a person who journals. This may be the perfect outlet for you to see the good that has transpired in your life that day. The more you are able to express thankfulness to people in your life and to your creator, the more good things you will begin to see happen. Usher in your freedom from violence; and rejoice.

Whenever things are not going right in my life, I do a check on my gratitude. I have seen bad things turn right by a change in my attitude. At the very minimum, every day that you wake up, you can be thankful that you have another day to pursue a fruitful life.

You will begin to see a difference in the people around you when you begin to acknowledge their contributions. Then, carry that a step farther; thank your creator for the people and opportunities that he places in your life. Never forget to *"Say What?! ..."* you are grateful for. Give praise to Him and allow others in your life know that there is an abiding thanks that you live with daily.

Remember: "Enter into his gates with thanksgiving, and into his courts with praise: be thankful unto him, and bless his name." Psalm 100:4

THE CONFESSION

The Lord my God is my everlasting light.

CHAPTER 19

You Are My Sunshine

Isaiah 60:19

The sun shall be no more thy light by day; neither for brightness shall the moon give light unto thee: but the LORD shall be unto thee an everlasting light, and thy God thy glory.

If you remember in Isaiah 59:9-10, God's people had separated themselves through their actions and dismissal of his ways. They looked for light and instead found obscurity, darkness. In their words...we stumble at noonday (a time of "double light" when the sun is at its highest point), as in the night.

What they were getting at was that when they had turned their backs on God, no matter how much physical light was available to them, their vision was impaired to the point that they could not see. When you have no spiritual light it is very difficult to make sound decisions.

It appears to me that one more time God's people, folks like you and me, had either through circumstance or over time lost touch with their trust in God's love for them. Perhaps it didn't start out as an outright thought…"oh, God doesn't know what He is talking about I'll just do it my way." But instead, they may not have taken time to hear and made a decision that they thought seemed good. Isn't that the way it is with us?

I can't begin to tell you how many times I have gotten off the beaten path, not seeing in the beginning that things were not working right. When the first glimmer of light would come in saying something wasn't right, I would try through my own devices to make things work.

We hate to be proven wrong! So when things aren't working right we hang in there longer than we should. All the while, our frustration level rises and peace, flees. And when it looked like there was no relief, through His mercy and grace…a little beacon of light begins to dawn.

Your internal conversation may sound like this, "Man! This thing is not working. If I'm not interested in total destruction; I need to get quiet, get with God to admit that my plan is not working and re-evaluate the situation."

This is what he did with his people in Isaiah 59:1. He started this return to him by saying to them, as he is saying to us this day, "Behold, the Lord's hand (power, means, direction) is not shortened, that it cannot save (be safe, to free), neither his ear heavy (burdensome, severe, dull), that it cannot hear."

When will we get to the point that we will no longer think of God as one of our sources but, our only source? When will we see a situation and the first thing we do is pray rather than saying as a last resort, "all we can do is pray?" When are we going to look at ourselves and decide that discipline and responsibility belong to us?

God will help us make the personal changes needed to make our lives and the life of our country. As a by-product, our contribution will be a building block to a healthy functioning world.

In your life you will find many forms of intellectual and spiritual enlightenment through experiences, tapes, documentaries, novels, movies, textbooks, relationships, and, yes, even television. Physical light comes from candles, electricity, sun, moon, and stars. No matter what form of light or enlightenment comes into your life it all has the same source. The source of all that you see and experience in this universe is your Creator.

If you open yourself up he will speak to you through all manner of media. I enjoy movies. I can't begin to tell you how many times I have received inspiration through movies and television. The farther you go along this path of life, the more you will see the lovely experiences and uncommon happenings are all tied into the One who orchestrates it all.

Acknowledgement His extraordinary power as the source of all the good things you see, hear, and intuit; is the beginning of having more and more revealed to you. People stop living when they stop learning new things. The older people that you see that are sharp and lively are those who have not stopped living their lives inquisitively.

Your Creator has made you with imagination and an inquisitive nature. He knows all things and desires you to know them also. All He asks is that you seek His counsel, talk to Him about everything. The answers to things you want to know are within your grasp. He prompts you with the scriptures.

> Mat 21:22 And all things, whatsoever ye shall ask in prayer, believing, ye shall receive.
>
> Luke 11:9 And I say unto you, ask, and it shall be given you; seek, and ye shall find; knock, and it will opened unto you.
>
> John 14:13 And whatsoever ye shall ask in my name, that will I do, that the Father may be glorified in the Son.

Creative ability is awakened when you begin to brainstorm with the most uncommon partner available. Open your mind and heart to the possibilities that He has made available to you. Look at the talents, gifts, and skills that He has placed within you.

Then ask where they can best be used. What area of life and its condition can you make better? Are you a troubleshooter? You need to be! We all have been designed to see a problem that we can solve. Just complaining about it doesn't cut it. Come to the table with a solution.

You have been placed here to solve a problem, help a person or a certain group of people. You may have one or several new products just waiting to spring onto the market. You may have one or several books lying just under the surface of your mind. You may be the next Warren Buffet or Bill Gates. You have dreams, ones that you may not have ever shared with anyone. Take courage. You have a partner who is there to guide you to success.

An interesting side note, you will probably first look to your strengths, talents, gifts and skills to fulfill that unique thing you were placed here to do. Don't be surprised if the problem you are inspired to solve needs attributes that you would consider beyond your natural ability. You need to take to heart the words in Philippians 4:13 that say "I can do all things through Christ which strengthens me."

It has been my experience that many of the times I have gone off the beaten path, when I messed up it was in areas where I was skilled, those areas with my greatest aptitude. In retrospect, I got cocky. You have to love the dictionary definition; to be annoyingly over self-confident. So, when I ran into a snag in the plan and there always seems to be a snag in the plan; I thought I could with my own devices fix what was happening.

The idea here is that you need to remember that you are here doing what you are doing with God as your partner. He knows how to do it best, how to maneuver out of tight spots, where you can help the most people and where you will get your greatest reward.

Your humility is not acting as if you have no skill or that your skill is not important but instead that you accept direction to use your skills properly, that you choose not to act alone. When you are lead to do something outside your comfort zone; take a leap of faith. He will help you succeed.

He is your everlasting light (to guide you and show you the way, to give you inspiration and understanding) and your glory (ornamentation, beauty, honor, embellishment).

THE CONFESSION

My mourning (I grieve no more, my joy is overwhelming) is at an end.

CHAPTER 20

Grieve No More

Isaiah 60:20

Thy sun shall no more go down; neither shall thy moon withdraw itself: for the LORD shall be thine everlasting light, and the days of thy mourning shall be ended.

Here is another instance where we find God repeating himself. This theme is carried forward from verse 19, stating that He is our everlasting light (illumination, happiness, luminous, very intelligent, beautiful, make something easier to understand).

God has become the means by which we see (understand) life and its varied circumstances, the people we meet and even ourselves. Only where there is wisdom and understanding about ourselves and our world can we with any certainty make right decisions to affect our families, communities, country and our world positively.

The more intimacy you develop in your relationship with God the more you will begin to see and understand. Secrets are shared between not associates (people who join others in some activity, or are frequently in the company of another) but close friends (a person you know well and regard with affection and trust).

In this very special relationship between you and the creator of the universe communication goes both ways. You will come to him with questions, problems and ideas. As you talk or journal these ideas through; he will not leave you adrift, but instead will open up (shed light on, give understanding, illuminate) answers to you. Inspiration will help you figure out how to proceed.

It has become clearer that he wants to share so much with us. As the creator of the universe, he wants to share His secrets with the family. It is his desire to make you aware of the ins and outs of relationships, business, politics, love, science; everything that affects your life. These answers and secrets are not revealed all at once.

A parent doesn't pour all the information they contain into their young child at one time. Instead, information is gradually released incrementally as higher levels maturity and ability to handle the information responsibly are proven. More information is divulged as trust is developed in that relationship.

Because parents love their children there is even information that is withheld until they can trust them with the heavy stuff. What God, your Heavenly Father, has for you is very good, real heavy stuff. Everything you ever need to know will be revealed in time.

The closer you draw to the true source of all of your wisdom, the more hope (earnest expectation) you will have for your future. Let's look at the word expect. It means to think something will happen, to think that it is reasonable, wait for something to arrive, consider due or obligatory.

Now if we consider something obligatory it must be done by rule or law, it is morally or legally binding. God has called us into a covenant with Him, which is a legally binding agreement that He cannot go back on. We can depend on it. He is not a man that He can lie.

Understand that the dreams and ideas that fuel your drive are given to you by Him. Ultimately, not only are dreams and ideas given to you by Him, but also the manifestation, actualization, or realization of these dreams in physical form. He reminds us in Psalm 37:4 to "Delight thyself also in the Lord; and He shall give thee the desires of thine heart."

Eventually, although you have had your trials along the road to manifesting what has been in your mind and heart, you will see that these bumps in the road have all played a part in making you a whole person. You become the person you were meant to be. Struggles are like a fire that refines ore, they make us stronger and more durable.

Without the strength you have gained during the trials in your life, your dreams might not survive. Although difficult while you are in the middle of them, weathered hardships help to give you another layer of Teflon coating. The next time a similar situation arises your response is smoother, problems don't stick to you like they used to.

This verse talks about a place after the trial where there is no longer a reason to cry in sorrow or grief; there are no more regrets. No more lamenting, showing publicly that you feel sad or disappointed. No more mourning, passionate and demonstrative activity of expressing grief. No more overwhelming sadness and pain.

In this place, the days of mourning are ended. Ended means to be in a covenant of peace, cause to be at peace, to be complete, be sound, make whole or good, restore, make compensation, or reward.

Repeatedly this chapter sings songs of victory; recovery from past hurts, injuries, and mistakes. Speaking these positive God inspired words over your life is one of the things that you can do to help build your faith.

You will begin to agree with the thoughts and plans of God for you and in all your future holds. See your future as if it were already here and say it as if it is already done. *"Say What?!..."* again and again! Believing is seeing!

THE CONFESSION

My people are all righteous. We inherit the land forever; the branch of your planting, the work of your hands, that you may be glorified.

CHAPTER 21

It Is Not About You Anyway

Isaiah 60:21

Thy people also shall be all righteous: they shall inherit the land for ever, the branch of my planting, the work of my hands, that I may be glorified.

He proclaims that not only you but your people (specifically a tribe, hence people, attendants, to associate) are all righteous. "Shall be" does not seem to be in the original Hebrew. These two words are written in italics, meaning these words have been inserted by the translators.

The statement in Hebrew transliteration is "Your people all righteous forever, will possess the land, the branch garden (planting) the work of my hands may be glorified (beautified)." This is a pretty great statement taken at face value. This is a simple statement with huge meaning.

He has planted you and your people here, at this time, promising that you and yours will possess the land (a particular place on the earth) forever. You are the work of his hand. You are glorified (beautified, an ornamentation) just like flowers are beautiful in the garden. You are his beauty and ornament in the place he planted you.

This statement also brings hope to you for those in your family who may not yet know the God that you talk about and love. Stand in agreement with His wish that they come to Him and allow Him to work in their lives, as He has worked in yours. Your relationship with him sanctifies them.

Now to me, this also includes those who are in your circle; friends, business associates, and tenants. All of these have the potential to be "your people," those who have been assigned to you. You will find that certain people are not in this circle, and are, therefore, not included in the "your people" category.

This is a good point in our discussion to talk about being selective about the people you allow hanging around in your inner circle. I bring this up because the people you choose to be with influence what happens in your life, your attitudes and even your financial well-being.

There are people that add to your life and you to theirs. Then there are those that are vampires; they are emotional, spiritual and financial vampires. These people will suck the life right out of you. When there is an indication that you need to break free from a certain person or group of people, do it.

Don't walk away from this relationship, run! You will be miles ahead. When someone or something that has a negative influence in your life leaves, there is now an opening for God to bring in those that will add value, not sap your energy.

There is a reason that your parents wanted to know whose family your buddies were from. They understood through experience that hanging around with people from a family that did not share their values and expectations for their children would be detrimental to you.

Some of you may have had the training from your parents to draw clear boundaries. Others may still have trouble drawing a line in the sand. For those of you who have trouble setting boundaries, do not worry, this is a skill that can be learned. Setting clear boundaries will be one of your most valuable tools.

As mentioned before, this is an area that I sorely lacked. Many of the troubles I've experienced in personal and business matters have been caused by an error in judgment regarding whom to allow close to me, whom to go into a venture with, and who should or should not be allowed to be close friends.

Although often warned by that still small voice and by friends and family members, rather than qualifying a newcomer I would naively jump headlong into one relationship after another. Giving too much too fast, trusting too much, and placing faith in someone based on their word. But, not verifying their ability and/or desire to follow through on what their spoken intent was.

If you want to go into business or personal relationship spend adequate time communicating. And then watch to see if they are a person who walks their talk. You cannot possibly insulate yourself from all hurt, however, there are steps you can take to walk with wisdom in relationship.

In my experience, there have been relationships that have been eliminated; either by my process, or theirs. Do not be surprised to see similar scenarios play out in your life. There are classifications of people that may be removed from your life. You may think only people who do you harm or mean you harm are wrong people.

Some folks who are in all other ways good folks will drain your resources if you let them in too close. They are, definitely, not the people talked about in this verse. Those who drain you in some way should be the first to be removed.

There are also perfectly outstanding people that will never play a part in your life and do not have a place in your inner circle. Some may at one time have been very close to you and through the passage of time or geographical change their role in your life has changed.

Only a select few will be in your inner circle, then others will be placed in other outlying rings of your circle. People outside this "my people" category are outside of your area of responsibility.

You were designed for a specific purpose. One of the problems we all encounter is that we are so busy earning a living, raising a family; waking, working and sleeping our days away that we do not know why we were placed here.

One of my favorite sayings is from the movie, The Last Samurai. Katsumoto asked Algren: "You believe a man can change his destiny?" And the answer from Nathan Algren: "I think a man does what he can, until his destiny is revealed."

This has always brought to mind two scriptures. The first is Job 8:7, "Though thy beginning was small, yet thy latter end should greatly increase." The second verse is Galatians 6:9, "and let us not be weary in well doing; for, in due season, we shall reap, if we faint not."

The point of this statement is that we may not know from an early age what our destiny is. However, at some point along our path that destiny is revealed, becoming clear to us. It does not mean that you just sit and do nothing until that time, but instead you make yourself useful in the meantime. All during this time you are developing in character and skills that will serve your purpose.

God's timing is perfection and in his time reveals your path to you. If you think you know your destiny, you may get tired of waiting; feeling that your dream is not happening fast enough. Unfortunately, it takes time. He works through you when you will allow it. Remain inspired by your dream, rehearsing it in faith.

There will be things that try to hinder your progress and break your focus. These things are all designed to make you freeze in place, so that you don't move forward. You will need courage and strength from above. Never quit, never stop. Inherit this land forever, the branch of His planting and the work of His hands.

In righteousness, you move forward. You meet each challenge, you accomplished each step toward inheriting your land, and then the fruit of this success is seen by others. They look at you, and they stand in awe. These fruits are a reward for you. Each new level of success brings glory to Him.

THE CONFESSION

A little one (my seeds) becomes a thousand and a small one a strong nation. You, Lord, hasten it (my 1000 fold) in your time.

CHAPTER 22

It's Harvest Time!

Isaiah 60:22

A little one shall become a thousand, and a small one a strong nation: I the LORD will hasten it in his time.

A little one (smallest quantity or thing, something cut off, detested or grieved) will become (this is always an emphatic statement, to be accomplished, required, to come to pass) a thousand (this word "eleph," an ox's head being the first letter of the alphabet, and was eventually used as a number – a thousand).

So, the smallest detested thing is required to become a thousand?! How can you not be excited about a little becoming a thousand times more than you sacrificed in the giving? And, a small one (something little in number, the least, the youngest, ignoble) a strong (powerful, great, and mighty; cause to increase) nation (a troop, nation or people) and I the Lord will hasten (hurry, be eager, with excitement, or enjoyment) in his time (sense of advancing, perpetuity).

How much more clearly can He paint this picture? This chapter finishes up with a statement of his desire for what he wants us to have, and that we aren't meant accomplish it in our own strength. He does not just help, this said He is making it happen.

This is one of the verses in the Bible that talks about the 1,000 fold harvest. The teachings in this Book are all about seed time and harvest time. Each word and deed is a seed for future harvest. The way you treat other people is a seed to the harvest of how you will be treated.

The finances you help a person or organization with are seeds to future financial harvests. Your conversations are seed. Your emotional input is a seed. Your love or anger is a seed. Each thought that you entertain; a seed to a future act.

What an extraordinary concept to think that each of these seeds brings forth harvest of the same kind. This comes about in the same way apple seeds grow apples. That harvest is a tree that produces approximately 1,300 apples per year.

If we use 500 pounds as the average yield per tree (trees go anywhere from 500-750 pounds yield per year), and the average apple weighs six ounces, we will come up with an average number of 1,300 apples per tree. Each apple has a minimum of two seeds and a maximum of ten seeds.

For every seed that grows into a tree it produces 1,300 apples to eat. With each apple producing the minimum of two seeds each; we would see an overall minimum yield of 2,600 seeds for planting. This is amazing because you would see an additional 3.3 million of apples in the years after these seeds were planted.

If this is a tree that is at its prime you could be looking at 750 pounds of apples, 2,000 apples, with even 6 seeds each; that would be 12,000 seeds as a harvest. This calculation is even more mind-boggling! You would see an additional 24 million of apples in the years after the seed from this first seed were sown.

That is from one seed planted! If we use only 10% of those seeds to replant, consider the increase that would produce. What if you chose to replant an additional 10%? How great would the harvest be from that crop?

Well, it works the same way in every other area of your life. He tells us in Matthew 6:30, "Wherefore, if God so clothe the grass of the field, which today is, and tomorrow is cast into the oven, [shall he] not much more [clothe] you, O ye of little faith?" Since He does this in the plant world, why should we expect anything less in our financial life?....in our relationships?....in our health?...in our business dealings?

You need to begin to think of yourself in larger terms, not as small and insignificant. We all begin small. This verse so significant because it is talking about God's children and their harvest; not that of a plant. You are that little one in the beginning, but with God backing you, you become mighty.

Some chapters in your life were probably detestable just as we spoke about earlier. Change begins to happen, your greatness begins to be increased as you ***"Say What?! ..."*** Continue sowing those seeds; speak a word of kindness to another, give even a small amount to someone in need or by sowing your time teaching someone something you know. No seed is too small to plant.

Your Heavenly Father sees these efforts and multiplies it back to you. Each act of sowing is an act of faith, in that it shows your belief in his word and his ways. Sowing into people and ministries and organizations; you are placing these acts of your life into the very hands of God and He makes you and what you do and what you have into something much greater.

It reminds me of teaching by Mike Murdock on the grasshopper complex. It doesn't take long in our lives for us to begin to see ourselves smaller than God's original intent. In the book of Numbers, there were twelve men who were sent to spy out the land of Canaan.

Ten of them believed that they were too small to do what God had placed in their heart to do. They openly said in Numbers 13:33, "And there we saw the giants, the sons of Anak (a Canaanite, a necklace…as if strangling, to choke, to collar), [which come] of the giants: and we were in our own sight as grasshoppers, and so we were in their sight."

Now this says that, first of all, they saw themselves as small, and then they assumed they were also seen this way in the eyes of the giants. This word giant means a bully, a tyrant, a feller (a person who fells trees). In those days, words and names meant more than they do now.

It is understandable why they were so freaked out by the thought of facing bullies and tyrants from a family whose name meant to choke. Please! But, and this is a big, but, they were not taking into consideration that the creator of the universe took them out of severe slavery and had promised them that they were leaders of their professions, communities and countries.

Are you ready to take your place? Are you willing to become; to advance with excitement and enjoyment? If so, you need to know that there will be giants to overcome.

Only two (approximately 16.7%) of the spies believed they could go in and take possession of this land. This is maybe the first example of the 80/20 rule in play. The 80/20 rule is considered the law of the vital few. That is how I see you, one of the vital few.

If you have read this far, you have a fire burning in your belly and desire to do great things. Do not allow your life to be sucked out. Operate in your dreams, your hopes. You have what it takes. Place yourself in God's hands, dare to believe that you are what He says you are and that you can do what He says you can do. Take time to dream big.

Remove the stress of excess busy-ness placed on you by yourself, your family, your job, and maybe even your church. Develop a plan to think. Dream again. Listen to that still small voice. Get clarity. Continue to *"Say What?! ..."* he has said about you and your life.

Then take one step at a time. Love others as you do yourself. Watch with eager excitement as the Lord makes you 1,000 times more and a great nation!

Finally, He has promised hasty fruit. My favorite meaning of hasten from the dictionary is excessively quick, speed up the progress of, and cause to occur rapidly. So, the Lord brings us an excessively quick occurrence of harvest.

In my walk, the thing that has most frequently caused delay is me! I got in the way at times with a lack of faith in the process or in not believing that he knows best, that he is always working for my good. I had fears that I couldn't do what he had whispered in my ear.

If these thoughts plague you, ask for help in removing those things that hinder your progress. And when He facilitates, making your way easier; give thanks and celebrate every victory, small or large! Remember to continue to *"Say What?! ..."*

Remember: "The Lord God of your fathers make you a thousand times so many more as ye are, and bless you as he hath promised you!" Deuteronomy 1:11

CONCLUSION

In wrapping up, I have seen a number of things occur in my own life that I cannot explain. I do not know all of the answers and wonder about people who claim they do. Over the years, there has been a lot of healing that has taken place for hurts both real and imagined. Healing often needs to take place before you begin to see the abundant realization of the dreams that have been placed in you.

NOTE: Keep in mind that the apple trees I used in an earlier chapter have their best fruit production between the ages of 10 to 30 years. Prior to that, fruit production can be sporadic and sparse. From my understanding, two things will affect more rapid production of trees; fertilization and pruning.

I liken fertilization to our study and meditation of the word, and pruning to the elimination from our lives of inappropriate people, wrong thought processes, and wrong actions through correction. Another fact that I found extremely interesting is that pruning (correction) during a dormant period will invigorate the tree to more production; however, summer pruning, when fruit is being born, will de-vigorate the tree, causing a slowing of tree growth.

I bring this up because we sometimes get discouraged by the lack of fruit (success) we may see early on in our quest for success. If you are experiencing this, take heart. Examine anything that may need to be changed, either by a change of heart and mind or in your environment, and the people you are allowing into your inner circle.

I have believed, since my early days as a believer in Christ, that it was necessary for me to personalize verses. Replace thee's and thou's with me's and you's. This helped make to the scripture more believable; more like He was talking directly to me, and in the process of this conversion, I took ownership of these promises.

Balance seems to be one of the keys. When we get out of sync in any one area, other areas begin to suffer. This is something I continue to struggle with, making progress and if not careful, falling back into imbalance.

Often people who are passionate have a problem keeping their lives in balance so take the time to evaluate where you are on occasion to make sure that you make whatever correction is needed to maintain balance and peace.

I have mentioned frequently the idea of giving (sowing). This may seem like a foreign concept to some of you, but look at it from the standpoint of your nine-to-five job. Until you plant the seed of your time and work, you will not receive that paycheck.

As you step out in faith, in giving, you will begin to see that you are able to do more with less. It is a paradox that I cannot explain. As you begin to spread around the finances that you have been given, you will see that whatever you have left over will go farther, and even beyond that; it will expand.

You will also find that there is a feeling of well-being that happens when you are able to help someone accomplish their goals. This could be an organization whose work you believe in or helping someone who may be struggling to keep their electric on. I think giving may be one of the legal forms of selfishness because, there is nothing that feels any better than giving to a worthwhile cause.

My life has changed so much because of the way that these verses have opened up to me. I hope that you find this as much of an adventure as I have.

ISAIAH 60 CONFESSION

I come today in dominion. I get up and decree guaranteed success, sure success. I am luminous. My heart and mind are illuminated. The clear thinking, understanding, and happiness of the Lord are streaming from me. Lavish outpouring (glory) of the Lord is appearing upon me and in my life.

I am heavy with riches. I am heavy with abundance. I am heavy with the splendor of wealth. I am heavy with magnificent copiousness.

Although there is darkness all around me, lavish outpouring is seen upon me and in my life by others.

Masses of people come to my clear thinking, understanding, and happiness; people of power, influence and position to the brilliancy of my appearance.

I am decked in gold and silver. My raiment is of fine linen and silk and embroidered work. I eat fine flour and honey and oil. I am exceedingly beautiful and prosper into a kingdom, and my renown (definite, appointed, purposed, lofty position marked by individuality, honor, authority and character) *goes forth among the nations for my beauty is perfect* (complete) *through your splendor* (glory) *which you put upon me.*

I lift my eyes and see! Masses of people unite and come to me. My sons (the builders of my house) come from far and wide. My daughters are supported and built up and have assurance at my side.

My eyes shine with joy, my heart thrills, for merchants from around the world flow to me, bringing me the wealth of many lands.

My hollows are filled with excess gold and incense that covers me. *I am wrapped in a heavy robe of wealth, and even though it is heavy, I am able to move more freely than ever before.* I am overwhelmed with being treated well and being done good to, beyond the usual and proper limits. Exaggerated, unrestrained and ornate resources are given to me. The hasty fruit of my seed, my 1,000-fold harvest (Midian and Ephah) is complete and comes to me now. (*This could come in the form of money, cars, transportation, accommodations, houses, jewelry, clothing, furniture, equipment, appliances, historical treasures, do-dads, and all other beautiful things.*)

All the flocks of men of mourning (Kedar) are given to me. The chiefs and strong support (rams) of increase, fruitfulness, and cheerfulness (Nebaioth) contribute to and serve me. They come with acceptance to Your altar.

Who are those who are unnoticed or hard to discern? And who has a lively, exhilarating spirit? Who are lurking? Who are afraid or don't know how to step forward? Show them to me; help me to help them succeed.
It is guaranteed that my islands, my coasts, and my desirable habitats earnestly expect me (THEY ARE WAITING FOR ME TO CLAIM THEM, and I claim them now)! My ships are coming in bringing my sons (the builders of my house) from afar, their silver and gold with them to satisfy every debt. The Holy one of Israel (known around the world) has glorified me (you bring me forth also with silver and gold, and there is not one feeble person in my family). You have given me this lavish outpouring (glory) in the eyes of all.

Foreigners' sons build my cities, obtaining more and more day by day. Presidents and kings send me aid (they minister to me, serve me). You have mercy on me, satisfying every debt (favor) through your grace.

You give me great and goodly cities that I built not (actual cities, apartment buildings, businesses, etc), houses filled with all good things that I filled not (you bring me houses and all their good contents, even surprise hidden wealth), wells dug that I dug not (equity, an ongoing well-spring of supply), and vineyards and olive trees that I planted not (other peoples harvest; I will tend those orchards and vineyards. This may show up as property, stocks, bonds, commodities, notes, businesses and/or anything else you choose).

My doors stay wide open around the clock to receive the wealth (the people, time, finances, resources) of many lands. Leaders of the world cater to me.

People and leaders who will not work for me will perish (wandering away and losing themselves), being utterly wasted.

The richness and honor (glory) of courage, understanding, feelings, wisdom, will, and intellect (Lebanon) come to me and are mine now. I am enduring, an instrument of war and of music, firm and straight, honest, happy, and prosperous all together. These attributes embellish the home of the Holy One. You make the place of my feet copious (rich).

Those who looked down on and browbeat me come bending to me, and all who abhorred and provoked me bow down at the soles of my feet. They call me a guarded city of the Lord, perpetually confident, strong, and victorious. You have made me so.

Where I was destitute and odious (an enemy) so that no one wanted to hang around with me, You have now hidden me from my enemies and have made me advance perpetually and given me victory without end.

Powerful kings and mighty people provide me with the choicest of their goods to satisfy my every need, and I know at last and really understand that You, the Lord, are my Savior and Redeemer, the Mighty One of Israel.

You exchange my brass for gold, my iron for silver, my wood for brass, my stones for iron (all of my resources are turned to silver and gold, spendable wealth). Peace and righteousness are my taskmasters.

Violence has disappeared from my land, wasting and destruction from my borders. My walls are salvation and my gates praise.

The Lord my God is my everlasting light. My mourning (I grieve no more, my joy is overwhelming) is at an end.

My people are all righteous. We inherit the land forever; the branch of your planting, the work of your hands, that you may be glorified.

A little one (my seeds) becomes a thousand and a small one a strong nation. You, Lord, hasten it (my 1000 fold harvest) in its time.

This is the perfect book for someone you know who is struggling financially, emotionally, and spiritually.

Visit **Say What!? – 'What' You Say is Your Future!** online at http://www.lindacnewberry.com for more information.

"After suffering a financial setback on one of my investments, I'd lost my desire to move forward with my plans. Linda and I got together, and after speaking with her, I was inspired to begin to build on my dream again. Now I'm back on track." - D'Nielle Suhuba-Baruti, President, BARE Investments LLC, Warren, Michigan

Yes, I want to give the gift of 'Say What!?' to my friends and family.

	Quantity	Price Each	Subtotal
Say What	_____	$14.97	_____
		Shipping	$5.00 per book
Please print legibly. Thank you!		Total →	_____

Name:_____

Address:_____

_____

Phone:_____

Email:_____

❏ MC ❏ Visa ❏ Discover Exp. Date:_____

Card Number:_____

Signature_____

Tarshish Productions

1933 N Stone Maple Ln

Elkhart, IN 46514

www.lindacnewberry.com/resources4urchg.html

info@lindacnewberry.com

Tarshish Productions

1933 N Stone Maple Ln
Elkhart, Indiana 47514

www.lindacnewberry.com

www.ingramcontent.com/pod-product-compliance
Lightning Source LLC
LaVergne TN
LVHW051829080426
835512LV00018B/2785